GOSPEL AND MISSION
IN THE WRITINGS OF PAUL

GOSPEL AND MISSION IN THE WRITINGS OF PAUL

An Exegetical and Theological Analysis

P. T. O'Brien

Baker Books

A Division of Baker Book House Co.
Grand Rapids, Michigan 49516

PATERNOSTER PRESS

CARLISLE, UNITED KINGDOM

© 1993, 1995 by P. T. O'Brien

First paperback edition, *Consumed by Passion*, published 1993 by Anzea Publishing, Homebush West, NSW 2140

Published by Baker Books
a division of Baker Book House Company
P.O. Box 6287, Grand Rapids, MI 49516-6287

and

Paternoster Press
P.O. Box 300
Kingston Broadway
Carlisle, Cumbria CA3 0QS
United Kingdom

Second printing, September 2000

Printed in the United States of America

For information about academic books, resources for Christian leaders, and all new releases available from Baker Book House, visit our web site:
http://www.bakerbooks/com

Library of Congress Cataloging-in-Publication Data

O'Brien, Peter Thomas
    Gospel and mission in the writings of Paul : an exegetical and theological analysis / P.T. O'Brien.
        p.   cm.
    Includes bibliographical references and index.
    ISBN 0-8010-2052-2 (pbk.)
    1. Bible. N.T. Epistles of Paul—Theology. 2. Paul, the Apostle, Saint—Contributions in the theology of missions. 3. Missions—Theory. 4. Missions—History—Early church, ca. 30-600. 5. Church history—Primitive and early church, ca. 30-600. I. Title.
    BS2652.027   1995
    225.9'2—dc20   95-16690

British Library Cataloguing-in-Publication Data

O'Brien, Peter T.
    Gospel and Mission in the Writings of Paul: Exegetical and Theological Analysis
    I. Title
    227.06

    ISBN 0-85364-614-7

Contents

ABBREVIATIONS

BAGD   Arndt, W. F., Gingrich, F. W., and Danker, F. W., trans. *A Greek-English Lexicon of the New Testament and Other Early Christian Literature*, by W. Bauer (2nd. ed., Chicago and London: University of Chicago Press, 1979).

BDF   Blass, F., and Debrunner, A., *A Greek Grammar of the New Testament and Other Early Christian Literature*, trans. and rev. R. W. Funk (Chicago and London: University of Chicago Press, 1961).

Bib   *Biblica*

BZ   *Biblische Zeitschrift*

IDB   Buttrick, G. A., ed. *The Interpreter's Dictionary of the Bible*, 4 vols. (Nashville: Broadman, 1962; supplementary volume, 1976).

JBL   *The Journal of Biblical Literature*

JETS   *Journal of the Evangelical Theological Society*

JSNT   *Journal for the Study of the New Testament*

JTS   *Journal of Theological Studies*

NIDNTT   *New International Dictionary of New Testament Theology*

NTS   *New Testament Studies*

RevExp   *Review and Expositor*

SPCIC   *Studiorum Paulinorum Congressus Internationalis Catholicus*, 2 vols. (Rome: Pontifical Biblical Institute, 1963).

TDNT   Bromiley, G. W., trans. and ed., *Theological Dictionary of the New Testament*, 10 vols. (Original German work ed. G. Kittel) (Grand Rapids: Eerdmans, 1964–76).

INTRODUCTION

The origin of this book can be traced to an Indian town in Maharashtra state several decades ago, when as a young missionary, along with several Indian and expatriate colleagues, I grappled with the problems of Christian evangelism in an area that had not been particularly responsive to the gospel. Church and mission leaders adopted a flexible approach as they sought to come to grips with the difficulties of proclaiming Jesus as Lord in that tough environment. Strategies changed regularly and, with each fresh attempt to present the saving work of the Lord Jesus more effectively, different Biblical texts (drawn mainly from the Pauline letters and the Book of Acts) were used to endorse these fresh policies. Instead of arguing on pragmatic grounds for these changes to their evangelistic program, either the explicit teaching or the example of the apostle was invoked to authorize them. A cycle of Pauline texts was used, with favourite verses being replaced by others as the strategies were modified—strategies which had obviously been determined on other grounds.

It seemed to one young missionary, at least, that there had to be a better way, and a careful study of the Pauline Epistles and the Book of Acts was called for, not least for the purpose of determining what elements of Paul's ministry, teaching and example were distinctive, and what characteristics he had in common with other Christians. Paul was a missionary, but a special kind of missionary—an apostle. What was unique to his apostleship? Did it have a special place in God's saving purposes, as so many claim? On the other hand, what features are continuous with our own context and which might serve as a model for other missionaries? Then too, what was Paul's understanding of his own mission? And how did this relate, if at all, to his teaching on mission generally.

The second catalyst for pursuing this subject occurred when our family returned home to Australia. At the time Christian leaders were concerned to stir up their fellow believers in the work of evangelism. All kinds of theological and pragmatic arguments were brought to bear on this worthy enterprise and a slender book, entitled *Move in for Action*, was produced at the time. But it soon became obvious that there were relatively few texts in Paul's letters urging believers in his churches to evangelize others. How does one explain this significant omission? I am grateful for the invitation to deliver the 1992 Annual Moore College Lectures for these have provided me with the opportunity of exploring, initially at least, several of these issues.

The Uniqueness of Paul in the Ancient World

At both the popular and scholarly levels Paul has had a special fascination for missionaries, whether in relation to his conversion, his methods and strategies, or his success. Over the years sermons have been preached about this missionary and countless writings, including some important monographs, have been produced in relation to his significance for the Christian mission.

There are very good reasons for this focus of attention on the missionary activity of Paul. According to Professor Martin Hengel of Tübingen, 'the success of the earliest Christian mission . . . was unique in the ancient world'. And with specific reference to Paul, Hengel adds: his 'mission [was] an unprecedented happening, in terms both of the history of religion in antiquity and of later church history. . . With Paul, for the first time we find the specific aim of engaging in missionary activity throughout the world'. As a result, what he did 'has remained unparallelled over the subsequent 1900 years'.[1] C. H. H. Scobie makes a similar point: 'The importance of Paul for the subsequent missionary expansion of the Church can scarcely be overemphasized. By his own extraordinary missionary activity concentrated into a relatively few years and by

---

1   M. Hengel, 'The Origins of the Christian Mission', in *Between Jesus and Paul. Studies in the Earliest History of Christianity* (London: SCM, 1983), 48, 49, 52.

the theology worked out in his letters Paul laid the foundations for the later expansion in both practice and theory'.[2]

A Fresh Paradigm: Approaching Paul as a Missionary Theologian

Although Paul's writings have been studied closely by missiologists, surprisingly the missionary dimension of his theology has not always been recognized. In the past he has been regarded as the creator of a dogmatic, theological system, as a 'mystic' (by the history-of-religions school), an 'ecclesiastic', or a biblical theologian—to name only a few approaches—but rarely understood by biblical scholars as an apostolic missionary.

Since the 1960s, however, there has been a paradigm shift and the notion that Paul was *both* a missionary *and* a theologian has gained ground among biblical scholars. N. A. Dahl, for example, who reported that Paul had been 'acclaimed as the first Christian theologian and as the greatest Christian missionary of all time', wrote about the need for integrating his theology and mission,[3] while Hengel argued powerfully that Paul was the first Christian theologian precisely because he was the first Christian missionary. The *Sitz im Leben* ('setting in life') of Pauline theology is the mission of this apostle.[4] So Robert Jewett claimed in 1988 that 'the awareness is dawning in current scholarship that Paul should be understood not simply as a theologian and writer of letters but as a self-supporting missionary actively engaged in cooperative projects with a number of groups and individuals'.[5]

---

2 C. H. H. Scobie, 'Jesus or Paul? The Origin of the Universal Mission of the Christian Church', in *From Jesus to Paul. Studies in Honour of F. W. Beare*, ed. P. Richardson and J. C. Hurd (Waterloo, Ont.: Wilfrid Laurier, 1984), 47. He adds: 'What Paul preached and practised was a universal mission. Clearly Paul sees himself playing the major role in proclaiming the Gospel throughout the whole *oikoumenē*' (48).

3 N. A. Dahl, 'The Missionary Theology in the Epistle to the Romans', in *Studies in Paul. Theology for the Early Christian Mission* (Minneapolis: Augsburg, 1977), 70. See also D. Bosch, *Transforming Mission. Paradigm Shifts in Theology of Mission* (New York: Orbis, 1991), 124, and others including M. Hengel, D. Senior, C. Stuhlmueller and A. J. Hultgren, whom he cites.

4 M. Hengel, 'The Origins of the Christian Mission', 49-50.

5 R. Jewett, 'Paul, Phoebe, and the Spanish Mission', in *The Social World of Formative Christianity and Judaism. Essays in Tribute to H. C. Kee*, ed. J. Neusner, E. S. Frerichs, P. Borgen and R. Horsley (Philadelphia: Fortress, 1988), 142.

Yet Paul's theology and mission do not simply relate to each other as 'theory' to 'practice'. It is not as though his mission is the practical outworking of his theology. Rather, his mission is 'integrally related to his identity and thought', and his theology is a missionary theology.[6]

It is my intention to take into account this paradigm shift in Pauline studies and to build on these recent insights in the hope that my analysis of Paul as a missionary will give us a greater understanding of his theology.

Limited Aims

This investigation of Paul has limited aims. First, it is my intention to discover what we can about his calling and commissioning, as well as the essential features of his ministry, including its goals, content, motivating power and results. In the process of doing this I shall explore what was distinctive about his missionary activity and how he understood his own mission. Paul was an apostle, a special kind of missionary. What was unique and unrepeatable about that calling? Among other things, this survey will involve us in coming to grips with the place of his missionary calling and ministry within God's redemptive purposes. Secondly, what did Paul *as a missionary* have in common with other Christians? Did he regard his own mission as related to the wider issue of mission? Hengel has claimed that Paul's missionary apostolate is so exceptional that it is not possible to emulate him.[7] Is this wholly true? Paul clearly expected his readers to emulate him in his goals, attitudes and behaviour. But was he in any sense a missionary paradigm and, if so, what are the characteristics of his model? For instance, was he an example to his converts in his commitment to gospel outreach?

So then, this inquiry is rather narrow. It is not intended to conduct an examination of Paul's strategies and methods, his plans and the place of his co-workers, as such, even though I am aware that many of these issues need to be addressed. However, it is hoped that some of the exegetical and theological conclusions

---

6   A. J. Hultgren, *Paul's Gospel and Mission. The Outlook from his Letter to the Romans* (Philadelphia: Fortress, 1985), 125, 145. Cf. F. Hahn, *Mission in the New Testament* (London: SCM, 1965), 97: Paul's 'view of the mission is inseparable from his entire theological thought'.

7   M. Hengel, 'The Origins of the Christian Mission', 52-53.

arising out of this more focussed study will throw light on these questions.

As Paul's understanding of his own mission and the theme of mission generally are surveyed, I shall limit my analysis to his letters. Luke's accounts of his colleague's missionary activities in the Book of Acts, while important for a comprehensive study of Paul as a missionary, will be used only in a supplementary way. Further, it has not been possible to make a comprehensive inquiry of all the relevant material in the apostle's letters. Instead, each chapter will focus on at least one major Pauline passage (with other supporting material) in order to throw light on the fundamental questions raised.

The first two chapters address the question of the distinctives in Paul's career as a missionary. In both of these the aim is to find out as much as one can about his understanding of his *own* mission. So in chapter 1 I shall look at two important passages (Gal 1:11-17; Eph 3:1-13) which deal with the significance of Paul's encounter with the risen Christ on the Damascus road. Chapter 2 focusses attention on Romans 15:14-33 where Paul describes the amazing effects of his missionary career.

The next three chapters attempt to take up issues common to him and other Christians. So chapter 3 investigates Romans 1:1-17 with the aim of determining Paul's involvement in the gospel and the place of the latter within God's saving purposes, before turning to the logic of Paul's gospel for men and women who have come under the lordship of Jesus Christ. It will be shown that the gospel is the bridge between Paul and contemporary Christians. If the gospel of the Lord Jesus is fundamental to Paul's understanding of his own mission it is also basic to his teaching on mission generally.

Chapter 4 addresses the issue of Paul as a godly example. In what senses is he a model and for what purposes? Particular attention is paid to his exhortation to follow his example as he follows that of Christ (1 Cor 11:1) in the context of 1 Corinthians 8:1—11:1. Chapter 5 raises the question as to why there is so little in the Pauline letters about the need for Christians to evangelize. Was it the apostle's intention that each new congregation should assume this responsibility? Some representative answers to these questions are presented and subsequently evaluated. The significance of Paul's language about the gospel's dynamic advance is addressed, while several examples of Christians actually engaging in evangelism are assessed as to their importance. Finally, the apostle's words about the spiritual warfare in Ephesians 6:10–20 and their implications for a dynamic proclamation of the gospel are probed.

A concluding chapter draws together the threads of this investigation and attempts to spell out both the meaning and the significance in both personal and strategic terms for contemporary mission and evangelism.

CHAPTER 1

THE MAKING OF A MISSIONARY

Converted, Called & Sent

Galatians 1:11-17; Ephesians 3:1-13

An important objective in this inquiry is to find out what were the distinctives of Paul's missionary apostleship and what features, *as a missionary*, he had in common with other Christians. The best way to approach this complex question is to focus, in the first instance, on what was unique and unrepeatable about Paul's missionary activity. How did the apostle understand his own mission? And what place did his missionary calling and ministry have within God's redemptive purposes? If by careful exegetical study we can arrive at some understanding of these distinctives, we will be less likely to make quick or superficial applications from the apostle's ministry or experience to our own lives and missionary strategies.

The place to begin this study is where Paul himself began, namely, his encounter with the risen and exalted Lord Jesus on the Damascus road. In this revelation of God's Son through the gospel Paul was converted, called and sent to the Gentiles. From this time on the course of his life was set.[1] He knew he had been sent as the chosen instrument of God for the Gentiles and he pursued this missionary goal with all the energy he possessed.

Paul's conversion/calling passages serve a variety of functions within his letters and not all of them are particularly relevant to our inquiry.[2] His personal testimony to the Galatian churches, given in

---

1   Among the many recent treatments on the significance of Paul's Damascus road experience see the important work of S. Kim, *The Origin of Paul's Gospel* (Grand Rapids: Eerdmans, 1982), as well as those of O. Haas, *Paulus der Missionar* (Münsterschwarzach: Vier Türme-Verlag, 1971), 5-26, M. Hengel, 'The Origins of the Christian Mission', 52-53, D. Senior and C. Stuhlmueller, *Biblical Foundations for Mission* (London: SCM, 1983), 165-171, and D. Bosch, *Transforming Mission*, 125-129.

2   S. Kim, *Origin*, 3-31, isolated the references and allusions in the apostle's letters to his conversion and calling on the Damascus road. They include Rom 10:2-4; 1 Cor 9:1, 16-17; 15:8-10; 2 Cor 3:4-4:6; 5:16; Gal 1:1, 11-17; Eph 3:1-13; Phil 3:4-11; Col 1:23-29, together with a number of opening verses of Paul's letters.

1

the context of opposition to both his gospel and his commission to preach it to Gentiles (Gal 1:11-17), is of cardinal importance for our study. We shall examine this passage first, and then turn to Ephesians 3:1-13,[3] before drawing together our conclusions.

Paul's Missionary Calling according to Galatians 1:11-17

> [11]I want you to know, brothers, that the gospel I preached is not something that man made up.[12] I did not receive it from any man, nor was I taught it; rather, I received it by revelation from Jesus Christ.[13] For you have heard of my previous way of life in Judaism, how intensely I persecuted the church of God and tried to destroy it.[14] I was advancing in Judaism beyond many Jews of my own age and was extremely zealous for the traditions of my fathers.[15] But when God, who set me apart from birth and called me by his grace, was pleased[16] to reveal his Son in me so that I might preach him among the Gentiles, I did not consult any man,[17] nor did I go up to Jerusalem to see those who were apostles before I was, but I went immediately into Arabia and later returned to Damascus.

In Galatians 1 we have Paul's first written account regarding his missionary commission. In it he provides important testimony about his calling to proclaim God's Son among the Gentiles and thus he throws light on his apostolic self-consciousness. From this significant evidence Paul shows he understands his gospel and missionary calling as follows:

(a) The gospel came by revelation to him on the Damascus road (vv. 11-12)

Paul reminds his readers of something which they had forgotten, namely, the nature and origin of the gospel. He asserts in a programmatic statement that his gospel was 'not according to man' (v. 11 NASB) and then supports this claim by referring to the source of the gospel and the manner of its coming to him (v. 12).

---

3   For reasons of space we have not included an examination of Colossians 1:24-29. Apart from the issue of Paul's suffering as an apostle and its relationship to his God-given task (vv. 24-25), other important features in the paragraph such as his commission in relation to the divine mystery and the place of the Gentiles within God's saving purposes have been taken up in relation to Ephesians 3:1-13. See further P. T. O'Brien, *Colossians, Philemon* (Waco, TX.: Word, 1982), 73-91.

He emphatically denies having received the gospel from any merely human source, either in general or from specific persons. He also denies that it came to him through the medium of teaching.

Rather, the gospel came (lit.) 'through a revelation of Jesus Christ', an expression which clearly refers to Christ's appearance to Paul on the Damascus road. Elsewhere he describes the event as a christophany: the Lord Jesus *appeared* to him (ὤφθη/*ōphthē*, 1 Cor 15:8; cf. Acts 9:17; 26:16), so that he could ask with confidence, 'Have I not seen Jesus our Lord?' (1 Cor 9:1). Paul regarded this christophany as of the same kind as the risen Christ's appearances to his disciples, and thus he counted himself among the witnesses to Jesus' resurrection (1 Cor 15:5-11).

The expression '[a revelation] *of* Jesus Christ' may indicate that the Lord Jesus was the revealer (a subjective genitive or one of origin).[4] But in the light of v. 16a, 'to reveal his Son in me', it is more probably objective, indicating that Jesus Christ was the one revealed. In other words, he was the content of the revelation.[5] God the Father was the revealer, Jesus Christ was revealed, and in that revelation Paul received his gospel. The gospel and the risen Christ were revealed to Paul in the same moment, for both were inseparable.[6]

Neither the noun 'revelation, disclosure' (ἀποκάλυψις/ *apokalypsis*) nor its cognate verb 'reveal' (ἀποκαλύπτω/ *apokalyptō*)— which belong to an important theological word group—ever describes a human activity or communication. Instead, these words speak of the revelation given by God,[7] Christ,[8] or the Holy Spirit,[9] or were the result of events brought about by them.[10] Often in Paul there is a def-

---

4   As the NIV renders it: 'by revelation from Jesus Christ'.

5   So many writers including F. F. Bruce, *The Epistle to the Galatians* (Grand Rapids: Eerdmans, 1982), 89, H. D. Betz, *Galatians* (Philadelphia: Fortress, 1979), 63, who claims that strictly speaking we do not have in 1:12 a '"self-revelation" of Christ because God does the revealing', E. Best, 'The Revelation to Evangelize the Gentiles', *JTS* 35 (1984), 16, and R. Y. K. Fung, *The Epistle to the Galatians* (Grand Rapids: Eerdmans, 1988), 54.

6   The revelation here in v. 12 is identical with, or at least coincident with, the revelation of God's Son in v. 16. This revelation of the gospel should not be taken to refer to the 'various revelations' mentioned in 2 Cor 12:1, which would make it subsequent to Paul's initial encounter with Christ.

7   Mt 11:25; 16:17; Gal 1:16; Phil 3:15.

8   Mt 11:27; Gal 1:12.

9   1 Cor 2:10; Eph 3:5.

inite emphasis on the disclosure of secrets of the last days. Here the reference is to a personal disclosure of Jesus Christ to Paul, a present revelation by God which anticipated the glorious unveiling on the final day: Christ was revealed to Paul in the form in which he will come at the end-time.[11] Paul saw Christ as the risen and exalted one in his glory.[12]

We shall have cause later on to examine in more detail the content of this gospel. For the moment, however, we note that the focus is on Christ Jesus himself, and that he was revealed to Paul by God.

(b) His conversion and calling were due to God's gracious initiative (vv. 15-16a)

If Paul's gospel came to him in his encounter with the risen Christ, then it was no less true to say that his commission to preach that gospel, and with it his apostolic authority, also came by special revelation from the exalted Lord. When he was confronted by Christ on the Damascus road, the gospel came to Paul (v. 12) and he was converted—although he doesn't actually use the language of conversion. Instead, he describes it as his calling through God's grace or his commission to preach Christ to the Gentiles (vv. 15-16).

Several scholars, since the ground-breaking work of K. Stendahl,[13] have argued that we should not use the word 'conversion' of Paul's Damascus road experience, since he did not change his religion, and he was neither tormented and guilt-ridden because of his sins, nor did he experience an inner conflict from which he needed to be delivered. However, while the stress here falls upon Paul's calling (καλέσας/*kalesas*, v. 15) and commission to the Gentiles (v. 16), the notion of 'conversion' is entirely appropriate to describe his Damascus road experience. What he speaks of in Galatians 1:11-17 includes his commission to the Gentiles, but it is not limited to it.

---

10   Especially the second coming: Rom 2:5; 8:19; 1 Cor 1:7; 1 Pet 1:7, etc.

11   J. Dupont, 'The Conversion of Paul, and Its Influence on his Understanding of Salvation by Faith', in *Apostolic History and the Gospel. Biblical and Historical Essays Presented to F. F. Bruce*, ed. W. W. Gasque and R. P. Martin (Exeter: Paternoster, 1970), 178, 192, and S. Kim, *Origin*, 56.

12   2 Cor 4:6; 1 Cor 15:43; Phil 3:21; cf. Acts 9:3; 22:6; 26:13. Cf. A. Wikenhauser, *Pauline Mysticism. Christ in the Mystical Teaching of St. Paul* (London: Nelson, 1960), 215, 'Paul saw the glory of God shining in the countenance of Christ'.

13   K. Stendahl, 'The Apostle Paul and the Introspective Conscience of the West', first published in 1963, now reprinted in *Paul among Jews and Gentiles* (Philadelphia: Fortress, 1977), 78-96. Note also the most recent article of J. D. G. Dunn, 'The Justice of God. A Renewed Perspective on Justification by Faith', *JTS* 43 (1992), 1-22, esp. 3-6, which argues along similar lines.

The language of v. 15, '[God] called (καλέσας/*kalesas*) me by his grace', refers not simply to his calling as *an apostle*, but also to his calling to be *a Christian* (see pp. 7–8), and thus into fellowship with God's Son, Jesus Christ (cf. 1 Cor 1:9). Further, from his testimony in Philippians 3:4-8 it is clear that a radical and dramatic change occurred in his thinking, indeed in his whole outlook. He no longer valued his earlier credentials, but regarded them as garbage because of his recognition of Jesus as the Messiah (vv. 7-8). The direction of his life was dramatically reversed and his convictions were turned upside down, not least in relation to the saving significance of the law. To speak of this encounter with the risen Christ as his 'conversion' is not only appropriate but also necessary.[14] For Paul, then, conversion and calling to preach the gospel coincided, though in Galatians 1 the emphasis falls upon the latter.

The apostle is quick to point out that his being called and sent was entirely due to *God's overwhelming gracious activity*. He shows this, first, by describing his former career in Judaism when he persecuted the church of God (vv. 13-14) and, secondly, by using several significant phrases which draw attention to the sovereign work of God, dating the first of these back to the time before he was born. Some of this language echoes that of the OT call narratives (e.g. Isa 49:1, 5; Jer 1:5) and we shall have cause to see later that Paul understood his missionary role to the Gentiles in terms of salvation historical fulfilment.

1. God set Paul apart before he was born (v. 15)

This first clause points to the divine activity of separating Paul to be a missionary before he was born.[15] The full phrase denoting

---

14   Note the detailed discussion of B. R. Gaventa, *From Darkness to Light. Aspects of Conversion in the New Testament* (Fortress: Philadelphia, 1986), 17-51. Cf. also D. Senior and C. Stuhlmueller, *Biblical Foundations*, 167-168; and D. Bosch, *Transforming Mission*, 125-126.

15   The verb ἀφορίζω (*aphorizō* 'to separate', 'set apart') was employed in the LXX mostly in a levitical or cultic sense to refer to the separation of part of a sacrifice (Exod 29:24, 26), the first-born (Exod 13:12), the leper (Lev 13:4, 5) or even Israel as a 'holy people' (Lev 20:26). At the heart of the NT notion of separation, for which there are OT precedents and models, we find the principle of God separating or marking off for his service. (Cf. K. L. Schmidt, *TDNT* 5, 454-455, for further references.) So Paul, as an apostle, knows himself to be 'separated for the gospel of God' (ἀφωρισμένος/ *aphōrismenos*, Rom 1:1). According to Acts 13:2 the Holy Spirit calls for the *setting apart* of Barnabas and Saul for the work to which they have been called. At Galatians 1:15 there is no purpose construction, as in the two references just cited, indicating the goal of Paul's being set apart. But the service which God had in view from this early time is made clear in the remainder of vv. 15 and 16: 'God was pleased to reveal his Son in me *in order that* (ἵνα/*hina*) I might preach him among the Gentiles'.

separation is: 'He [i.e. God] who set me apart from my mother's womb'. This expression which was rooted in the call narratives of the OT (Isa 49:1, 5; Jer 1:5; cf. Judg 16:17; Pss 22:11; 71:6), stresses the uninterrupted connection with God 'from my birth' or even 'before I was born' (RSV). Because of this and other OT echoes in Galatians 1:15, it has been claimed that Paul describes his being sent as an apostle to the Gentiles in terms of the Servant of the Lord and (possibly) of Jeremiah.[16]

Although there is some difference of opinion, we agree that Paul echoes the language of Jeremiah in Galatians 1:15-16, since the prophet's experiences are akin to Paul's 'apostolic self-consciousness'.[17] Jeremiah knew that his call from Yahweh had been a true experience and that his message was God's sure word to Israel. But how could he prove that he was a true prophet who stood in the council of the Lord and had heard his word (Jer 23:18-22) when the false prophets had not? The validity of Jeremiah's commission was bound up with the truthfulness of the Lord's message. Similarly, the validity of Paul's commission was also questioned. Attempts were made to undermine his apostolic standing in the eyes of his converts. In the final analysis Paul's commission and the gospel he preached were inextricably linked. To denigrate one was to despise the other. Paul, like Jeremiah, had 'stood in the council of the Lord', that is, he had received both his gospel and his commission to preach it from the risen and exalted Lord Jesus.

Paul's allusion to Isaiah suggests that he was chosen by God to continue the work of the Servant of Yahweh.[18] The Servant knew that he had been set apart by Yahweh from birth (Isa 49:1, 5). This choice from the beginning had a positive ministry to Gentiles in view: 'I will give you as a light to the nations, that my salvation may reach to the end of the earth' (v. 6). Further, the Servant's ministry was wholly dependent on Yahweh's calling of him (49:1). Paul's description in Galatians 1:15-16 highlights each of these

---

16　See the recent discussion of K. O. Sandnes, *Paul—One of the Prophets?* (Tübingen: Mohr, 1991), 48-70.

17　Note the arguments of F. F. Bruce, 'Further Thoughts on Paul's Autobiography (Galatians 1:11–2:14)', in *Jesus und Paulus. Festschrift für W. G. Kümmel zum 70. Geburtstag*, ed. E. E. Ellis and E. Grässer (Göttingen: Vandenhoeck, ²1978), 23-25, and cf. R. Fung, *Galatians*, 63-64.

18　Cf. R. Fung, *Galatians*, 63-64.

elements: choice from before his birth, calling and a ministry to Gentiles.

In drawing on this Isaianic language Paul is not suggesting that he was the new servant of the Lord. Rather, his ministry is modelled on and a continuance of that of the Servant who had been set apart by the Lord from birth with a specific ministry to Gentiles in view. Other references to the Isaianic Servant of the Lord in Paul's letters suggest that the apostle saw his missionary role as tied in with this salvation historical figure.[19]

2. He called Paul by his grace (v. 15)

If the first clause referred to the divine activity of separating Paul to be a missionary, then the second speaks of God's sovereign action in calling (καλέσας/*kalesas*) him. This second work of God is neither the same as the separation from before his birth nor coincident with it.[20] Instead, it describes what happened on the Damascus road when God was pleased to reveal[21] his Son in Paul.

But to what does this language of calling refer: Paul's summons from God to be an apostle, as the vast majority of commentators suppose, or the divine call to be a Christian, as the καλέω/*kaleō*-terminology frequently signifies in his writings? In the immediate context 'called' could be taken either way and, in fact, I think Paul is speaking of both. He often uses the verb καλέω/*kaleō* to describe God's historic calling of men and women to salvation[22] (Rom 8:30; 1 Cor 1:9; 7:15; Gal 1:6; 5:13; 2 Tim 1:9), and includes himself along with other Christians when he writes about God having called '*us*' (Rom 9:24; 1 Thess 4:7). The cognate adjective 'called' (κλητός/*klētos*) is employed in a two-fold sense of believers as 'called

---

19 Cf. Romans 15:21 with Isaiah 52:15; 2 Corinthians 6:2 with Isaiah 49:8; Romans 10:16 with Isaiah 53:1; note also Acts 13:47 with Isaiah 49:6, and Acts 18:9, 10 with Isaiah 43:5. On the wider use of the Servant language in relation to Paul's ministry see W. Radl, 'Alle Mühe umsonst? Paulus und der Gottesknecht', in *L'Apôtre Paul*, ed. A. Vanhoye (Leuven: Leuven UP, 1986), 144-149. In relation to earlier debates see also the discussion of W. P. Bowers, *Studies in Paul's Understanding of His Mission* (unpublished Ph. D. dissertation, Cambridge, 1976), 137-143.

20 Although the two participles ἀφορίσας/*aphorisas* ('separated') and καλέσας/*kalesas* ('called') are conjoined by the one definite article ὁ/*ho*, this is because the subject of the two actions (i.e. God) is the same, not because the separation and calling are identical or coincident in time.

21 'Called' and '[pleased to] reveal' are coincident. See most recently R. Y. K. Fung, *Galatians*, 64.

22 On 'calling' in Isaiah see 41:9; 42:6, 11; 43:1; 45:3; 48:12, 15; 49:1; 50:2, etc.

ones' (Rom 1:6, 7; 8:28; 1 Cor 1:2, 24) and of an apostle as 'a called one' (Rom 1:1, etc.).

At the same time, the significant theological term 'grace' (χάρις/*charis*) which appears in our text, 'he called me through his *grace*', is employed in a similar twofold manner. It describes, on the one hand, God's gracious activity on behalf of men and women in bringing them to salvation in Christ (1 Cor 1:4, etc.) and, on the other, his calling of Paul to be an apostle. Indeed, on some occasions 'grace' can be synonymous with 'apostleship' (Rom 1:5; cf. 1 Cor 3:10; 15:10; Gal 2:9).[23]

There appears, then, to be a parallelism between the 'calling' terminology (καλέω/*kaleō* and κλητός/*klētos*) and that of 'grace' (χάρις/*charis*). Both are employed of the salvation event in Christ, the former with reference to God's calling men and women to salvation, the latter of his gracious movement in Christ towards humanity. And both terms have particular reference to Paul's calling as an apostle to the Gentiles.

So when Paul speaks of being 'called through his [*sc.* God's] grace' he is referring to his calling *both* as a Christian *and* an apostle,[24] though the latter stands to the fore. In the light of his past behaviour when he persecuted the church of God (v. 13), such a calling could only be due to God's gracious activity. Paul knows that he is unworthy to be either a Christian or an apostle (1 Cor 15:9). *Grace* indicates this. But it also suggests, in the light of the above, that his calling to be an apostle to Gentiles is bound up with the salvation event itself.

3. God was pleased to reveal his Son in Paul (vv. 15-16a)

The reason for the remarkable change in Paul's life is now given: God was pleased to reveal his Son in him. For Paul calling and revelation coincided in time. The divine call 'was presented to Paul in the form of a manifestation of God's Son'.[25]

---

23   Note the discussion of A. Satake, 'Apostolat und Gnade bei Paulus', *NTS* 15 (1968-69), 96-107.

24   F. F. Bruce, *Galatians*, 92, notes that at v. 6, where God is the one 'who called you in grace', the 'general call of God to all his people is in view'; at v. 15 'that is included, but it involves also the special call of God to Paul for his personal life-work'. Cf. D. Wiederkehr, *Die Theologie der Berufung in den Paulusbriefen* (Freiburg, Schweiz: Universitätsverlag, 1963), 87.

25   J. Dupont, 'The Conversion of Paul', 178.

The reference to the divine good pleasure (εὐδοκέω/*eudokeō*)[26] draws attention to God's gracious initiative and absolute sovereignty in making known his Son, while the statement that the revelation was *in me* is deliberately intended to stress 'the inward and intensely personal character of God's revelation to him of the risen Jesus'.[27] In fact, 'in me' underlines 'the inwardness already implied by the verb "reveal", which connotes a disclosure involving perception and understanding on the part of the recipient'.[28] This is not to suggest, however, that the revelation was merely inward without a corresponding external object, for the preceding phrase ('to reveal his Son') refers to Paul's vision of the risen Christ on the road to Damascus (cf. v. 17). For Paul the outward vision and the inward illumination coincided.[29]

The risen Christ appeared to Paul on the Damascus road as *God's Son* (υἱός/*huios*), that is, the content of the revelation was Jesus as the Son of God. In recent years Seyoon Kim has brought the importance of Paul's Damascus road experience for an understanding of his faith and theology back to the centre of the discussion.[30] Kim's claim is that crucial emphases in Paul's gospel, especially his Christology, soteriology and universal mission, were formed in large measure in that encounter itself. The gospel which Paul received on the Damascus road, and thus the content of his preaching, may be defined christologically: it is Jesus Christ, the Son of God (Gal 1:12, 16; cf. 2 Cor 4:4; Eph 3:8) who is the crucified, risen and ascended Lord.

---

26   C. Dietzfelbinger, *Die Berufung des Paulus als Ursprung seiner Theologie* (Neukirchen-Vluyn: Neukirchener Verlag, 1985), 61, suggests that the freedom of God's gracious choice is underlined by this verb.

27   M. J. Harris, *NIDNTT* 3, 1191, is one of many scholars taking this line.

28   R. Y. K. Fung, *Galatians*, 64.

29   E. Best, 'The Revelation to Evangelize the Gentiles', 1-30, esp. 16. Vision and revelation are closely linked in 1 Corinthians 15:58, while at 9:1 the objectivity of the vision is presented 'as guaranteeing the authenticity and hence the validity of Paul's vocation'; so R. Y. K. Fung, *Galatians*, 64. F. F. Bruce, *Galatians*, 92, makes the important point: 'The appearance of the risen Christ to him was an objective experience, in which Christ took the initiative: the repeated ὤφθη of 1 Cor 15:5-8 ("he let himself be seen") means that the appearance of the risen Christ to him was as real as his earlier appearances to Peter, James and others, not that their experiences were as "visionary" as Paul's'.

30   S. Kim, *The Origin of Paul's Gospel*.

(c) The purpose of his missionary commission was to preach God's Son among the Gentiles (v. 16b)

God's gracious *purpose* (ἵνα/*hina*) in revealing his Son in him was that 'he might preach him among the Gentiles'. This was an integral part of the revelation itself.[31] When Paul refers back to the Damascus road christophany his missionary calling *to the Gentiles* is often in view: he was entrusted with the gospel of the uncircumcision (Gal 2:7; 1 Thess 2:4), having 'received grace and apostleship to bring about the obedience of faith among all the Gentiles' (Rom 1:5). Paul was given grace by God to be a minister *for the Gentiles* in the priestly service of the gospel (Rom 15:15-16). The 'logic of the gospel according to Paul' required that he should proclaim the Son of God to the nations and he grasped the essentials of it there and then. This is not to deny that his convictions about this calling grew or that he came to a deeper understanding of the magnitude of his missionary task. But the main lines of Paul's preaching Christ to the Gentiles were already set at the time of the Damascus road revelation. That he seems to have entered his ministry without delay serves to confirm this.

(d) Paul's commission and salvation history

One of our aims in this inquiry has been to determine what was unique to Paul's service as an apostle and, on the other hand, what features he held in common with other Christians. Paul was a missionary, but a special kind of one, an apostle to the Gentiles, and before we conclude our study of Galatians 1:11-17 we need to understand the place of his apostolic commission within God's saving purposes. Two important points need to be made in relation to this: the first concerns his gospel, the second his commission to preach it.

(1) Galatians 1:11-12 presents a programmatic statement which introduces the nature and origin of Paul's gospel.[32] As he begins his autobiographical section (v. 13) he harks back to his encounter with the risen Christ on the Damascus road and emphasizes (a) the

---

31   See Appendix A.

32   G. W. Hansen, *Abraham in Galatians. Epistolary and Rhetorical Contexts* (Sheffield: Academic Press, 1989), 98. He adds that this is the 'thesis statement' of the letter which is 'elaborated by the autobiographical section and the Abraham argument in roughly parallel fashion'.

revelatory origin of the gospel (1:16; cf. 1:12; 2:2), (b) its christological centre (1:15-16; cf. v. 12) and (c) the mission to the Gentiles (1:16; cf. 2:2, 7-8). According to G. W. Hansen, Paul uses an extended and parallel argument based on the Abraham story (3:7ff.), first, 'to authenticate and validate the authority of the revelation to him'; secondly , 'to show its consistency with his gospel'; thirdly, 'to defend his mission to the Gentiles' and, finally, to 'destroy the opponents' biblical basis for compelling the Gentiles to judaize'.[33]

Of particular importance for our purposes is the *identification* of *that gospel* with the *promise* to Abraham: Galatians 3:8, 'And the scripture, foreseeing that God would justify the Gentiles by faith, declared the gospel beforehand (προευηγγελίσατο/*proeuēngelisato*) to Abraham, saying, "All the Gentiles shall be blessed in you."' Having made this identification Paul develops a description of the promise (3:14, 16-19, etc.), but in the process he continues his definition of the gospel. And just as the *gospel* has been spoken of in terms of benefits to Gentiles, so the *promise* is related to blessings for them (3:8, 14, 29; 4:28).[34]

Thus, the gospel which Paul received on the Damascus road when he was confronted by the risen Christ may be identified with the promise made to Abraham in which blessings will be extended to Gentiles. As Paul preached that gospel and Gentiles were brought into a covenant relationship with the living God through faith, so the promises made to Abraham were in the process of being fulfilled.

(2) In the light of our discussion above we have concluded that Paul's analogy with Jeremiah reflects his 'apostolic self-consciousness',[35] while his allusion to Isaiah suggests that he was chosen by God to continue the work of the Servant of Yahweh. The Servant knew that he had been set apart by Yahweh from birth (Isa 49:1, 5). This choice from the beginning had a positive ministry to Gentiles in view: 'I will give you as a light to the nations, that my salvation may reach to the end of the earth' (v. 6). Further, the Servant's ministry was wholly dependent on Yahweh's calling of him (v. 1). Paul's description in Galatians 1:15-16

---

33   G. W. Hansen, *Abraham*, 99.

34   G. W. Hansen, *Abraham*, 84.

35   F. F. Bruce, 'Further Thoughts', 23-25.

highlights each of these three elements: choice from birth, calling and a ministry to Gentiles.

In drawing on this Isaianic language Paul is not suggesting that he was the new servant of the Lord. Rather, his ministry is modelled on and a continuance of that of the Servant who had been set apart by the Lord from birth with a specific ministry to Gentiles in view. Other references to the Isaianic Servant of the Lord in Paul's letters suggest that the apostle saw his missionary role as tied in with this salvation historical figure.

Therefore, in Galatians 1:11-17, where Paul's gospel is defined both christologically and in terms of his mission to the Gentiles, two significant points are made about his missionary calling and salvation history. First, the gospel which came to him by revelation on the Damascus road and which he now preaches (Gal 1:11-12, 16) is described in terms of God's promise made to Abraham (Gal 3:8). God's salvation historical purposes linked to Abraham are now being fulfilled as Gentiles are brought into a living relationship with him through that gospel. Secondly, Paul's missionary commission to proclaim God's Son among the Gentiles is spoken of in language that suggests he is continuing the important salvation historical work of the Servant figure of Isaiah 40-55.

The Divine Mystery and Paul's Stewardship. Ephesians 3:1-13

> [1] For this reason I, Paul, the prisoner of Christ Jesus for the sake of you Gentiles— [2] Surely you have heard about the administration of God's grace that was given to me for you, [3] that is, the mystery made known to me by revelation, as I have already written briefly. [4] In reading this, then, you will be able to understand my insight into the mystery of Christ, [5] which was not made known to men in other generations as it has now been revealed by the Spirit to God's holy apostles and prophets. [6] This mystery is that through the gospel the Gentiles are heirs together with Israel, members together of one body, and sharers together in the promise in Christ Jesus. [7] I became a servant of this gospel by the gift of God's grace given me through the working of his power. [8] Although I am less than the least of all God's people, this grace was given me: to preach to the Gentiles the unsearchable riches of Christ, [9] and to make plain to everyone the administration of this mystery, which for ages past was kept hidden in God, who

created all things. [10] His intent was that now, through the church, the manifold wisdom of God should be made known to the rulers and authorities in the heavenly realms, [11] according to his eternal purpose which he accomplished in Christ Jesus our Lord. [12] In him and through faith in him we may approach God with freedom and confidence. [13] I ask you, therefore, not to be discouraged because of my sufferings for you, which are your glory.

In Ephesians 3:1-13, our second passage for study, Paul harks back once more to the Damascus road event. This time, however, he speaks of the revelation of the mystery to him (v. 3) and God's grace given to him so that he might preach the unsearchable riches of Christ to the Gentiles (v. 8). The two elements found in Galatians 1, namely, the revelation of Christ in the gospel and the commission to preach him, appear in the same sequence in Ephesians 3, though now in terms of 'the mystery' and Paul's administration of it within God's purposes.

Paul understands his gospel and missionary calling in Ephesians 3 along the following lines:

(a) Both his gospel and his commission to preach it were wholly determined by and dependent upon God's grace (vv. 2, 7 and 8).

It is surprising how often in the context of his ministry to Gentiles that Paul speaks of the marvellous grace of God given to him. In this paragraph he goes out of his way to underscore that grace in a most emphatic way: he uses not only the terms 'grace' (χάρις/*charis*, vv. 2, 7 and 8) and 'gift' (δωρεά/*dōrea*, v. 7), but also the verb 'give' (δίδωμι/*didōmi*) on three occasions (vv. 2, 7 and 8) when, strictly speaking, it was redundant. In addition to this, the whole passage focusses on the divine kindness to Paul and the Gentiles who are recipients of 'the boundless riches of Christ' (v. 8).

1. His stewardship of God's grace (v. 2)

As in Galatians 1 (cf. Rom 1:5; 15:15) so here also Paul emphasizes that he is a recipient of God's grace. He speaks of 'the stewardship' (οἰκονομία/*oikonomia*) of that grace, by which he means not the grace of apostleship (which is mentioned in v. 7 and developed in vv. 8-12) but 'the grace of God embodied and proclaimed in the gospel'.[36] Obviously, the two are closely linked. But just as in Galatians 1 Paul dealt first with the revelation of the gospel (vv. 11-12) and then with his commission to preach it (vv. 15-17), so here too in Ephesians 3 he focusses first on God's revelation to him of the mystery regarding the Gentiles' part in salvation (vv. 2-7) before spelling out the means by which this goal is achieved,[37] namely, by his enlightening them about this mystery (vv. 8-12). Divine grace was not given for Paul's personal enhancement. Instead, it was for the sake of the Gentiles, as the following words, 'for you', show.

2. A minister of the gospel because of God's grace (v. 7)

Having spoken of the revelation of the mystery *to him*, the apostle now turns his attention to the preaching of the mystery *through him*. The saving purposes of God involved not only a revealing of the gospel mystery to Paul, but also the pressing of him into the service of that gospel.[38]

He became a 'servant' (διάκονος/*diakonos*) of the gospel (cf. Col 1:23) when he was converted on the Damascus road and this point is supported by the aorist tenses 'became' (lit. 'was made') and [the grace] 'given' (cf. vv. 2, 8). Paul's calling to be a missionary to the Gentiles was not of his own doing. Instead, it was wholly due to the gracious, sovereign intervention of God. He who was so conscious of his own unworthiness, because he had been an opponent of that gospel, points out this deeply held personal truth in a most emphatic way. First, he indicates he 'was made' a minister of the gospel *by God*,[39] and, secondly, he heaps up expressions for divine grace and power: 'gift', 'the grace of God', 'given to me', 'working' (ἐνέργεια/*energeia*) and 'his power' (δύναμις/*dynamis*). The cause of his reception of this commission to proclaim the

---

36 F. F. Bruce, *The Epistles to the Colossians, to Philemon, and to the Ephesians* (Grand Rapids: Eerdmans, 1984), 311. (It is called 'the good news of God's grace' in Acts 20:24.) On this view τῆς χάριτος/*tēs charitos* ('of grace') is an objective genitive (so most commentators) or a genitive of content.

37 C. C. Caragounis, *The Ephesian Mysterion. Meaning and Content* (Lund: Gleerup, 1977), 74.

38 S. Kim, *Origin*, 24.

39 Assuming the passive of the verb (ἐγενήθην/*egenēthēn*) is to be pressed. It then signifies a 'creation by God rather than a deployment of man's own resources', according to M. Barth, *Ephesians 1-3* (Garden City, NY: Doubleday, 1974), 339.

gospel, which he regarded as the highest honour indeed, was 'the gracious gift which God imparted to me'.[40]

In the final phrase of v. 7, 'through the working of his power', Paul makes two additional points that throw further light on his understanding of his calling to the missionary task and its execution. First, 'through the working of his power' is linked with '[God's grace] given to me'.[41] God's gracious gift to Paul, by which he was called to be a servant, was due to the effective working of divine power. 'The grace experienced by Paul in his ministry flowed out of the mighty power of God'.[42] Just as nothing short of God's mighty intervention could transform him from being a persecutor into a Christian, so it took that same almighty and effective working to make him into a 'servant of the gospel'.

Secondly, since both 'working' and 'power' in other contexts draw attention to the ongoing mighty work of God, then this would suggest that the apostle is focussing here not only upon God's powerful working in grace to *commission* him. The expression also points to his ever-present consciousness that day by day he experienced 'the operation of his power' in the *fulfilment* of his missionary calling. It was not only in God's initial call but also in the subsequent enabling that he knew of the divine power operating mightily within him. This is the explicit point he makes in the parallel passage, Colossians 1:29, and elsewhere in his writings, notably 1 Corinthians 15:10:

> But by the grace of God I am what I am, and his grace to me was not without effect. No, I worked harder than all of them—yet not I, but the grace of God that was with me.

We therefore find in Ephesians 3:2-7 the recurring emphasis that everything Paul has become and achieved in his apostolic mission is 'not his own doing, but the result of God's grace—God's choice of him, God's call to him, God's enabling power'.[43] And in the exercise

---

40 F. F. Bruce, *An Expanded Paraphrase of the Epistles of Paul* (Palm Springs, CA: Haynes, 1981), 273. δωρεά/*dōrea* is the '*gift, bounty* of God' (BAGD, 210), and χάριτος/*charitos* ('of grace') is a genitive of quality or definition.

41 Most commentators contend, rightly in our judgment, that the two κατά/*kata*-phrases in the verse are not coordinate.

42 A. T. Lincoln, *Ephesians* (Dallas: Word, 1990), 182.

43 C. L. Mitton, *Ephesians* (London: Oliphants, 1976), 124.

of his apostleship to the Gentiles 'he gave practical effect to the divine plan made known to him by revelation'.[44]

3. Grace enables him to proclaim the unsearchable riches of Christ to the Gentiles (v. 8)

As he reflects on his commission to be Christ's missionary to the Gentiles Paul is filled with amazement at the extraordinary privilege that has been given to him. Using a very striking expression in which he neither indulges in hyprocisy nor grovels in self-deprecation,[45] he indicates how deeply conscious he is of his own unworthiness and of Christ's overflowing grace to him: 'to me who am less than the least of all God's people' (NEB) has this grace been given. As if the superlatives 'least' (among the apostles, 1 Cor 15:9) or 'first and foremost' (of sinners, 1 Tim 1:15) were insufficient to express his unworthiness, Paul creates a new form of this Greek adjective, that is, a comparative of a superlative (ἐλαχιστότερος/*elachistoteros*, 'leaster', 'less than the least').[46] He remembers here his violent persecution of the church *of God*[47] (1 Cor 15:9). His repeated, specific references to his role as a persecutor reveal his consciousness of sin.[48]

But the paragraph is not dominated by the notion of Paul's unworthiness, real though this was. He had experienced the amazing grace of God and so he goes out of his way to emphasize it. In this instance 'the grace given' was that grace which enabled him to discharge his missionary commission, although one needs to realize that this 'special' grace was part and parcel of the comprehensive grace by which he became a Christian. Further, God worked effectively in Paul's life since his own unworthiness did not hinder him from assuming his missionary responsibilities in relation

---

44   F. F. Bruce, *Ephesians*, 317.

45   J. R. W. Stott, *God's New Society. The Message of Ephesians* (Leicester: Inter-Varsity, 1979), 119.

46   Cf. BDF §60(2), 61(2), and A. T. Robertson, *A Grammar of the Greek New Testament in the Light of Historical Research* (Nashville: Broadman, 1934), 278, 670.

47   The words 'of God' stresses the enormity of the crime: it was *God's* church that Paul sought to destroy.

48   Note M. Barth, *Ephesians 1-3*, 340, who adds: 'because this awareness has a specific focus, it is distinct from a possibly morbid preoccupation with himself or with sin in general. His self-humiliation is unlike the expression of hidden pride and its concomitant fishing for compliments'. Cf. O. Haas, *Paulus*, 19.

to the Gentiles. He set about fulfilling this task energetically, profoundly aware that God had called him to it.

This grace given to Paul consisted in his 'bringing the Gentiles the good news of Christ's unfathomable wealth'. This impressive expression describes an activity of proclamation, the content of which is both glorious and comprehensive.

(b) Integral to Paul's missionary calling is the divine mystery

Three times within the space of a few verses in Ephesians 3 (vv. 3, 4 and 9) Paul employs the highly-charged theological term 'mystery' (μυστήριον/*mystērion*) when speaking of his missionary calling.[49] Usually mystery in his letters refers not to some future event that lies hidden in God's plan, but to his decisive action in Christ here and now. In Ephesians 3 Paul focusses first on God's revelation to himself of the mystery regarding the Gentiles' part in salvation (vv. 2-7) before spelling out the means by which this goal is achieved,[50] namely, through the privileged task he has received to enlighten them about this mystery (vv. 8-12).

The apostle speaks of the content of this 'open secret' in terms of Gentiles being incorporated along with Jews into the body of Christ and states that it is through the gospel that this marvellous purpose of God is achieved (v. 6). As he reflects upon his commission to be Christ's missionary to the Gentiles, Paul is amazed at the extraordinary privilege which has been given to him of preaching the unsearchable riches of Christ to the Gentiles (v. 8). But this was not all. His missionary commission included a second element which has both a salvation historical and a personal dimension to it—not as something additional or unrelated to the proclamation of the gospel but integral to it. Paul had the privilege of bringing to light for all to see how this hidden purpose of God was being put into effect.[51] As men and women responded in faith

---

49 Understood against its OT background, particularly the Book of Daniel (where it corresponds to the Aramaic *rāz*, 'secret', Dan 2:18, 19, 27, 28, 29, 30, 47|[twice]), this μυστήριον/*mystērion* denotes 'an eschatological mystery, a concealed intimation of divinely ordained future events whose disclosure and interpretation is reserved for God alone', G. Bornkamm, *TDNT* 4, 814-815; cf. R. E. Brown, *The Semitic Background of the Term 'Mystery' in the New Testament* (Philadelphia: Fortress, 1968), 8.

50 C. C. Caragounis, *Mysterion*, 74.

51 The infinitival expression 'and to enlighten' (φώτισαι/*phōtisai*), v. 9, is not an expansion or amplification of the infinitive 'to preach [the unsearchable riches]' (εὐαγγελίσασθαι/*euangelisasthai*) of v. 8. C. L. Mitton, *Ephesians*, 125, speaks of Paul's proclaiming the gospel in such a way 'that its implications were unmistakably clear, so as to make all men see God's unfolding plan'.

to the preaching of the gospel and were incorporated into the Lord Jesus Christ, so it became evident as to how God was blessing Gentiles along with Jews in fulfilment of the promises made to Abraham (Gen 12:2-3). The OT prophets had already looked forward to the saving purpose of God in which Gentiles along with Israelites would be embraced within its scope. But the *manner* in which that purpose would come to fruition—by incorporation of both Jews and Gentiles into the body of Christ (v. 6)—had not been made known. *This* had remained a mystery until the time of its fulfilment and Paul, as the apostle to the Gentiles and first steward of this mystery, has the privilege of unfolding its wonder to his readers.

(c) Paul's calling and God's ultimate purposes

So then, in Ephesians 3:1-13 Paul makes it clear that his missionary calling to preach the gospel to Gentiles is an integral part of God's redemptive plan. This point emerges, not through the apostle's language echoing that of the OT as in Galatians 1, but because of his relationship with the mystery and its administration (vv. 2, 3, 4, 8 and 9). The broad sweep of God's salvation historical plan is in view when the term 'mystery' is used at Ephesians 3:1-13 (as read in the light of 1:3-14), while important features of its content are emphasized in v. 6. Gentiles are recipients of the divine promise to Abraham (Gen 12:1-3); they are fellow-heirs because they are heirs of God and fellow-heirs with Christ (Rom 8:17). OT promises regarding the divine indwelling through God's Spirit also find their fulfilment in these Gentiles who are partakers of the promised Holy Spirit in Christ Jesus (Eph 1:13; 2:18; 4:30). These promises come to fruition through the gospel which Paul preaches.

The grand design[52] of God's salvation historical plan was that 'now, through the church, the manifold wisdom of God should be made known to the rulers and authorities in the heavenly realms' (v. 10). A new multi-racial community was 'taking concrete shape before people's eyes'[53] and in it the wisdom of God was being displayed. The resulting new humanity of Jews and Gentiles as fellow members of the body of Christ was 'to serve throughout the

---

52   The ἵνα/*hina*-clause probably denotes purpose:'so that'.

53   J. R. W. Stott, *Ephesians*, 123.

universe as an object-lesson of the wisdom of God'.[54] The instrumentality of the church in this disclosure of the divine wisdom had nothing to do with any special additional task that the people of God were to engage in, be it evangelism, social action, or the like. Paul's phrase means nothing other than that the *church itself* is the manifestation of the hidden secret. 'The establishment of the Church, which is the working out of the divine mystery, is the tangible evidence of this [hidden secret]'.[55]

The salvation and unity of Jew and Gentile in Christ had always been integral to the divine purpose. The God in whom this 'mystery' was previously hidden from eternity is 'the Creator of all things' (v. 9). His creation of heaven and earth was an important step in the fulfilment of that purpose. And more recently, the apostle's preaching the unsearchable riches of Christ (v. 8) and bringing to light the administration of the long-hidden mystery (v. 9) had as their goal the grand object of this salvation historical plan, namely, that the manifold wisdom of God should be made known to the principalities and powers (both good and bad alike) in the heavenly places through the church (v. 10).

Conclusions

We began by examining an important question of interpretation, namely, the issue of what was unique to Paul's missionary calling—as an apostle he was a special kind of missionary. Because Paul's encounter with the risen Christ on the Damascus road ultimately set the course for the remainder of his life, and his calling formed the basis of his theology, we turned to Galatians 1 and Ephesians 3 to ascertain his understanding of that calling and whether it had any significance within salvation history. This was part of a wider concern to discover what he thought of his own mission and how this fitted, if at all, into his teaching on mission generally.

---

54 F. F. Bruce, *Ephesians*, 320. M. N. A. Bockmuehl, *Revelation and Mystery* (Tübingen: Mohr, 1990), 203, comments: 'as the visible evidence of the mystery of Gentile incorporation into the Messianic community . . . [the church] is well suited to serve as a manifestation of God's inscrutable saving wisdom to the hitherto ignorant angelic powers'.

55 R. E. Brown, *Background*, 60. Cf. H. Merklein, *Das kirchliche Amt nach dem Epheserbrief* (München: Kösel, 1973), 214.

The following conclusions and implications emerge from our study:

(1) The gospel which came to Paul was a personal disclosure of Jesus Christ, a revelation of God which anticipated the glorious unveiling of his Son on the final day (Gal 1:11-12, 15-16). Paul saw God's Son as the risen and exalted one in his glory. Although the means by which this gospel was received by Paul was distinctive, that is, it came by a personal appearance of the Lord Jesus, its content was not unique to him. It was the same message which he was commissioned to proclaim among the Gentiles so that they too might be converted and brought into a living relationship with the Lord Jesus.

From a salvation historical perspective this gospel which he preached is identified with the promise made to Abraham (Gal 3:8). As the apostle proclaimed the kerygma and Gentiles were brought into a covenant relationship with the living God through faith, so the promises made to Abraham were in the process of being fulfilled.

We ought not to expect that Christians generally or missionaries in particular will experience a personal disclosure of Jesus Christ in the way that Paul did. But the gospel of the Lord Jesus which he received and which he was so eager to proclaim to others is for all who believe, Jew and Gentile alike.

(2) God had set Paul apart for his service before he was born. Echoing OT prophetic call language, he speaks of this divine separation in terms that suggest he was conscious, like Jeremiah, that he had stood in the council of the Lord and that his message was God's sure word to the Gentiles. At the same time Paul's allusions to Isaiah (49:1, 5, 6) suggest that he was chosen by God to continue the work of the Servant of the Lord. Both had been chosen from birth, both were wholly dependent on Yahweh's calling, and both had a positive ministry to Gentiles in view.

This feature of Paul's service was distinctive and unrepeatable because of his place within God's saving plan. However, in a secondary sense it may be appropriate to speak of us who proclaim the gospel as continuing the Servant's ministry since we declare what the Lord's chosen one has done for us and we call others to embrace the benefits of his saving work.

(3) Paul was deeply conscious of his own unworthiness. He goes out of his way again and again to emphasize God's sovereignty and

gracious initiative in calling one who had been a persecutor to himself and his service. Together Galatians 1 and Ephesians 3 make it plain that Paul's receiving the gospel, his calling to minister to the Gentiles and his ability to fulfil his missionary task from beginning to end were due solely to the grace of God. Obviously some of these features were distinctive to the apostle. However, the notion that his ministry from start to finish was due to divine grace is consistent with his teaching about spiritual gifts elsewhere (1 Cor 12:1-11). We do well to remember that as we engage in the task of speaking about Jesus as Lord we, like Paul, are wholly dependent on God's grace and kindness to us.

(4) We saw in Ephesians 3:1-13 that Paul's missionary calling to preach the gospel to the Gentiles was an integral part of God's redemptive plan. This truth was brought out clearly with his use of the key theological term μυστήριον/*mystērion* (God's 'open secret'), which in its context showed that the salvation and unity of Jew and Gentile had always been integral to the divine intention. The OT prophets had already looked forward to the day when Gentiles along with Israelites would be embraced within the sphere of divine blessing. How this would come about—by incorporation of both Jews and Gentiles into the body of Christ—had not been made known. This had remained a mystery until the time of its fulfilment and Paul, as the apostle to the Gentiles and first steward of this mystery, had the privilege of unfolding its wonder. His missionary commission included two elements: (a) the preaching of the unsearchable riches of Christ (v. 8) and, as an integral feature of that proclamation, (b) the bringing to light for all to see how this hidden purpose of God was being put into effect (v. 9). As he engaged in this task the divine promises were being fulfilled and awaiting their consummation.

Clearly, as the apostle to the Gentiles, Paul's relationship to the 'mystery' was unique. However, through his writings we have come to know the content of God's saving plan for Jews and Gentiles: it is through the proclamation of the unsearchable riches of Christ that both can be incorporated as fellow-members into his body. As we faithfully present the gospel to men and women of any race, class or creed and they receive the divine message for themselves, so God's marvellous promises to Abraham continue to be fulfilled.

Appendix A. When Was Paul Commissioned to Go to the Gentiles?

The question has been raised as to whether Paul's commissioning had the Gentiles in view *from the very beginning*, or whether the full significance of the Damascus road christophany came to him later or emerged in his thinking over a period of time. In other words, was the purpose 'therefore to the Gentiles' part of the Damascus road revelation itself or not?

J. Dupont answers in the negative and asserts: Paul 'did not claim that Christ had given him the command to evangelize the Gentiles and there is nothing to allow us to imagine that this injunction was given him explicitly at this time'.[56]   Similarly, E. P. Blair, among others, contends that the ἵνα/*hina*-clause (*hina*, 'in order that') of v. 16 reflects Paul's understanding of the purpose of the christophany at the time of writing Galatians, but tells us nothing as to when he was called to the Gentile mission.[57]

Instead, it has been claimed that: either (a) this element, 'therefore to the Gentiles', was first imparted to Paul in a subsequent vision (cf. Acts 22:21), or (b) he saw the risen Christ enthroned at God's right hand and subsequently, through meditating on the OT Scriptures, interpreted the christophany as his call to be an apostle to the Gentiles,[58] or (c) Paul thought of himself as called to be an apostle, without further specification, and only later concluded that his apostleship was to the Gentiles, or (d)

---

56   J. Dupont, 'The Conversion of Paul', 193. M. S. Enslin, H. Schlier and F. Mussner also take this line.

57   E. P. Blair, 'Paul's Call to the Gentile Mission', *Biblical Research* 10 (1965), 23; cf. R. Liechtenhan, *Die urchristliche Mission. Voraussetzungen, Motive und Methoden* (Zürich: Zwingli, 1946), 78, and J. Jeremias, *Der Schlüssel zur Theologie des Apostels Paulus* (Stuttgart: Calwer, 1971), 26.

58   So O. Betz, 'Die Vision des Paulus im Tempel. Apg. 22, 17-21, als Beitrag zur Deutung des Damaskuserlebnisses', *Verbonum Veritas. Festschrift für G. Stählin*, ed. O. Böcher and K. Haacker (Wuppertal: Brockhaus, 1970), 113-123, believes that Jeremiah 1:4-10; Isaiah 49:1-6 and especially 6:1-13 provided the key for the right interpretation of the Christophany and this involved his calling to be an apostle to the Gentiles. But as S. Kim, *Origin*, 57 n. 3, rightly contends, Paul's interpreting the Christophany and his call in the light of these Old Testament texts 'does not necessarily preclude Paul's hearing the commissioning words from Christ who appeared to him.   Having heard Christ's call in the Christophany, Paul would naturally have turned to the Scriptures and meditated upon the texts of the prophetic calls in order to see the significance of his call in the light of them'.

he first began as a missionary to the Jews and then gradually became conscious of his sending to the Gentiles.[59]

There are, however, decisive reasons for believing that Paul's commission to the Gentiles was part of, indeed an essential ingredient of, the revelation on the Damascus road:

First, when Paul's words of Galatians 1:15-16a are read in conjunction with what immediately follows, they show that he was convinced he should go to the Gentiles from the beginning, and that he held this conviction before he met the other apostles. His commission owed nothing to them for it was rooted in the Damascus christophany (1:11, 12).[60]

Secondly, in the polemical context of Galatians 1 and 2, unless Paul had been conscious of his calling to preach Christ among the Gentiles from the beginning, he could hardly have said with confidence that 'the Christophany had the purpose of commissioning him specifically for the Gentile mission'. Had that conviction with its law-free Gentile mission dawned on him only later he might well have been asked why he had not given any prior evidence of such a calling. Indeed, he could have been charged with interpreting his conversion experience as God's call— and only later at that! Would not this prove that he was a self-made 'apostle'?[61]

Thirdly, the christophany on the Damascus road constituted for Paul both his gospel and his commission to preach it to Gentiles. When he refers back to this event his missionary calling to the Gentiles is frequently in view: so he 'was entrusted with the gospel' (1 Thess 2:4), 'the gospel of the uncircumcision' (Gal 2:7). He 'was set apart for the gospel of God' (Rom 1:1), through Jesus Christ the Lord he 'received grace and apostleship to bring about the obedience of faith among all the Gentiles for the sake of his name' (Rom 1:5), he was given grace by God to be a minister for the Gentiles in the priestly service of the gospel (Rom 15:15-16),

---

59 Note S. Kim's criticisms of this view, *Origin*, 58-64.

60 R. Y. K. Fung, *Galatians*, 66, and J. D. G. Dunn, '"A Light to the Gentiles": the Significance of the Damascus Road Christophany for Paul', in *The Glory of Christ in the New Testament. Studies in Christology*, ed. L. D. Hurst and N. T. Wright (Oxford: Clarendon, 1987), 251, 252; note also his arguments on the significance of the verbs used in 1:16 and 18 in 'The Relationship between Paul and Jerusalem according to Galatians 1 and 2', *NTS* 28 (1982), 462-466.

61 S. Kim, *Origin*, 59.

and sent by Christ to preach the gospel (1 Cor 1:17). Paul can speak directly of his compulsion to preach the gospel which is laid upon him (1 Cor 9:16), that he is a debtor to Greeks and barbarians (Rom 1:14) and that he had been grasped by Christ on the Damascus road (Phil 3:12). As H. Kasting has rightly pointed out, the manifold nature of the expressions only serves to present the same basic thrust: Paul's calling is to preach the gospel and this to Gentiles, for he is 'the apostle of the Gentiles' (Rom 11:13).[62]

We conclude, then, that the purpose of the revelation on the Damascus road—that Paul should preach Christ among the Gentiles—was part of the revelation itself.[63] The logic of 'the gospel according to Paul' required that he should proclaim the Son of God to the nations and he 'grasped this in essence there and then'.[64] Of course, this is not to deny that Paul's convictions about his calling grew or that he came to a deeper understanding of the magnitude of his missionary task.[65] We know from Philippians 3:7-11, in relation to the Damascus road encounter, that Paul's deep-seated resolution to submit to Jesus as Lord had fuller implications to which he gladly responded (cf. v. 8 with v. 7). Further, it was his great ambition to know Christ more and more (v. 10), and this will have involved a fuller appreciation of Jesus' rule over the nations and with it a deeper understanding of his Master's heartfelt compassion for the lost (note the Servant's mission of Isa 52:15 which Paul takes up in support of his pioneer policy of preaching the gospel where Christ had not been named, Rom 15:21). But the

---

62　H. Kasting, *Die Anfänge der urchristlichen Mission* (München: Kaiser, 1969), 56-57; cf. F. F. Bruce, *Galatians*, 93, S. Kim, *Origin*, 57-59, and J. D. G. Dunn, 'A Light', 251-253. Paul's use of the 'mystery' motif, according to Dunn, reinforces this same point. The mystery for Paul meant God's purpose to bring the Gentiles into the people of God (Rom 11:25). Indeed, one may express its goal in terms of '*the obedience* of faith' for all the Gentiles (Rom 16:26). In his initial commissioning Paul was given the ministry of making known 'the riches of the glory of this mystery among the Gentiles' (Col 1:26-27; cf. Eph 3:2-9).

63　On the issue as to whether Paul *heard* this commission from Christ, see S. Kim, *Origin*, 57-58, and O. Betz (discussion above); cf. J. D. G. Dunn, *Jesus and the Spirit* (London: SCM, 1975), 97-114. Questions that arise are: What actually happened? Did he actually see Jesus? Was it verbal as well?

64　F. F. Bruce, *Galatians*, 93; cf. J. D. G. Dunn, 'A Light', 251-253. R. Liechtenhan, *Die urchristliche Mission*, 77, aptly remarked: 'Paul did not entertain any doubt that he had been called to be the apostle to the Gentiles' from the time of the Damascus christophany.

65　Cf. M. Hengel, 'Origins of the Christian Mission', 49-54, F. F. Bruce, *Galatians*, 93, and S. Kim, *Origin*, 60-61.

main lines of Paul's preaching Christ to the Gentiles were already set at the time of the Damascus road revelation. That Paul seems to have entered his ministry without delay serves to confirm this.

CHAPTER 2

THE AMAZING SUCCESS OF PAUL'S MISSION

Romans 15:14-33

In the first chapter we directed our attention to two significant passages in Paul's letters (Gal 1:11-17; Eph 3: 1-13) which focus on his calling and commission as a missionary to the Gentiles. Our aim in analyzing these texts was to determine what elements of his ministry were distinctive. A further and related aim was to discover the place of Paul's gospel and missionary calling within the purposes of God. Our concern was to find out all that we could about his understanding of *his* own mission. This attempt to analyze Paul's theology of *his* mission was part of a broader inquiry into his *theology of mission* generally.

As part of our ongoing study of the distinctive elements of Paul's ministry, we now turn to Romans 15:14-33, especially vv. 14-21, where the apostle gives a brief overview of his missionary career from its beginnings to the present—a period of more than twenty years—and describes its amazing effects. At this important turning point, the conclusion of his missionary endeavours in the east, Paul provides significant insights into what he had been doing and what were his hopes for the future.[1] He thus throws light on essential features of his ministry, including its goals and motivating power, its content and extraordinary results, as well as his all-consuming ambition to proclaim Christ where he had never been heard. We learn a great deal about Paul's missionary activity and how it fitted into the saving purposes of God. The apostle writes to the Roman Christians with a sense of fulfilment (v. 19), using spatial categories

---

1   W. P. Bowers, *Studies*, 15. Cf. also D. W. B. Robinson, 'The Priesthood of Paul in the Gospel of Hope', in *Reconciliation and Hope. New Testament Essays on Atonement and Eschatology presented to L. L. Morris on his 60th Birthday*, ed. R. J. Banks (Exeter: Paternoster, 1974), 231-245.

to focus on the geographical dimension of his mission ('from Jerusalem and as far round as Illyricum'). He speaks of a missionary involvement in the proclamation of the gospel that led to the establishment of settled congregations, and all of this was set within an eschatological frame of reference in which divine blessing had come to the Gentiles in fulfilment of OT expectation.[2]

Some Distinguishing Marks of Paul's Mission

[14] I myself am convinced, my brothers, that you yourselves are full of goodness, complete in knowledge and competent to instruct one another. [15] I have written you quite boldly on some points, as if to remind you of them again, because of the grace God gave me [16] to be a minister of Christ Jesus to the Gentiles with the priestly duty of proclaiming the gospel of God, so that the Gentiles might become an offering acceptable to God, sanctified by the Holy Spirit. [17] Therefore I glory in Christ Jesus in my service to God. [18] I will not venture to speak of anything except what Christ has accomplished through me in leading the Gentiles to obey God by what I have said and done— [19] by the power of signs and miracles, through the power of the Spirit. So from Jerusalem all the way around to Illyricum, I have fully proclaimed the gospel of Christ. [20] It has always been my ambition to preach the gospel where Christ was not known, so that I would not be building on someone else's foundation. [21] Rather, as it is written: 'Those who were not told about him will see, and those who have not heard will understand.'
[22] This is why I have often been hindered from coming to you. [23] But now that there is no more place for me to work in these regions, and since I have been longing for many years to see you, [24] I plan to do so when I go to Spain. I hope to visit you while passing through and to have you assist me on my journey there, after I have enjoyed your company for a while. [25] Now, however, I am on my way to Jerusalem in the service of the saints there. [26] For Macedonia and Achaia were pleased to make a contribution for the poor among the saints in Jerusalem. [27] They were pleased to do it, and indeed they owe it to them. For if the Gentiles have shared in the Jews' spiritual blessings, they owe it to the Jews to share with them

---

2   W. P. Bowers, *Studies*, 172. These three dimensions—the geographical, the ecclesiological and the eschatological—are the particular concerns of Bowers' analysis.

their material blessings. [28] So after I have completed this task and have made sure that they have received this fruit, I will go to Spain and visit you on the way. [29] I know that when I come to you, I will come in the full measure of the blessing of Christ.

[30] I urge you, brothers, by our Lord Jesus Christ and by the love of the Spirit, to join me in my struggle by praying to God for me. [31] Pray that I may be rescued from the unbelievers in Judea and that my service in Jerusalem may be acceptable to the saints there, [32] so that by God's will I may come to you with joy and together with you be refreshed. [33] The God of peace be with you all. Amen.

Although Romans 15:14-33 was thought by earlier writers to be simply part of Paul's epilogue or personal narrative that rounds out the epistle, and therefore relatively unimportant, recent scholarship has shown that this paragraph is integral to the whole letter and has several important functions within it. The main body of Romans is a treatise on Paul's gospel (see chapter 3).[3] This body is bracketed by an epistolary opening (1:1-17) and conclusion (15:14–16:27), in which 15:14-33 plays an important part, stressing this motif of the 'gospel'. The emphasis on Paul's mission to the Gentiles (15:16) flows from the detailed argument of the letter as a whole; it is the theological corollary of Paul's exposition of the gospel and God's saving purposes for both Jew and Gentile. 'Paul wrote as he did [in this paragraph] because he had been given the gospel for the Gentiles, and his ministry was crucial to the completion of God's plan of salvation; hence the need both to explain his gospel and to promote it'.[4] Referring to this passage D. W. B. Robinson stated: 'Paul cannot separate his own role from the operation of the gospel which he thus expounds to his Gentile readers in Rome. Romans is both an exposition of the gospel of hope and at the same time Paul's *apologia* for his "priesthood" in that gospel'.[5]

Even a cursory reading of this paragraph makes it plain that Paul has used highly significant language to make some important statements about the nature of his missionary endeavours, his understanding of his own mission to the Gentiles and the saving

---

3   D. Moo, *Romans 1-8* (Chicago: Moody, 1991), 28.

4   J. D. G. Dunn, *Romans 9-16* (Dallas: Word, 1988), 856.

5   D. W. B. Robinson, 'The Priesthood of Paul', 232.

purposes of God. Once again he draws attention to the priority of divine grace. He then employs OT cultic language, Exodus terminology, an OT quotation and the language of mission in order to draw attention to essential features of his ministry.

(a) The priority of God's grace in Paul's missionary career (v. 15).

We have already seen from Galatians 1 and Ephesians 3 that Paul's calling and sending as a missionary were wholly dependent upon divine grace. An overwhelming sense of God's unmerited favour is again to the fore in this paragraph where Paul surveys his missionary career up to the present and describes its effects. He speaks once more of the Damascus road experience in the words, 'the grace that was given to me by God' (v. 15). Paul knew from the time of his conversion onwards (note the aorist δοθεῖσαν/*dotheisan*, 'given') that his ministry as a missionary apostle was due to God's mercy alone. And it was the *whole of his missionary career*, not just his calling or commissioning, that was due to the overwhelming grace of God (it is all of v. 16 that is dependent on this key expression): divine mercy provided the source and power for the whole course of his ministry.[6]

(b) The content and goal of his missionary activity (v. 16).

In a remarkable utterance, which finds no exact parallel elsewhere in the NT, Paul makes a profound statement about the nature of his commission and its relationship to salvation history, the gospel and, by implication, to the Roman Christians themselves. He makes these issues clear as he sets forth the purpose of God's gracious gift to him:

> [Divine grace was given to me] to be a minister of Christ Jesus to the Gentiles in the priestly service of the gospel of God, so that the offering of the Gentiles may be acceptable, sanctified by the Holy Spirit.

There is a concentration on OT cultic terminology in this statement that is quite exceptional as Paul describes his special apostleship to the Gentiles by means of the metaphor of the priestly

---

6   K. F. Nickle, *The Collection. A Study in the Strategy of Paul* (London: SCM, 1966), 135-136. Cf. O. Haas, *Paulus*, 30.

cult. First, he speaks of the *content* of the ministry to which he was called as 'the priestly duty (ἱερουργοῦντα/*hierourgounta*)[7] of proclaiming the gospel of God'. He acts on Christ's behalf by discharging his priestly responsibilities in relation to the cult itself, namely, the gospel of God.

Then Paul refers to the *purpose* of his commissioning and thus of his whole missionary career: it is '*in order that* the offering (προσφορά/*prosphora*) of the Gentiles might be acceptable to God, sanctified by the Holy Spirit' (v. 16). There is some difference of opinion as to the meaning of the phrase, 'the offering of the Gentiles'.[8] On balance, it seems best to regard the cultic language as having two perspectives: the offering is the Gentiles themselves and this is epitomized in the material gifts brought by their representatives to meet the needs of the Jerusalem leaders. Accordingly, this unusual phrase refers to *both* the Gentiles *and* their gifts.

The implication of this statement of purpose is that Paul's missionary activity is 'out in the world' rather than in the Temple. At the same time the offering itself 'breaches the fundamental distinction between Jew and Gentile which prevented Gentiles from even getting near the great altar of sacrifice in the Temple'.[9] In response to the criticism of the Judaizers that his Gentile converts were 'unclean' because they were uncircumcised, the apostle asserts that this sacrifice of the Gentiles is pleasing to the living God because (1) he has acted decisively to make it acceptable (behind the verbal form in the expression 'that the offering of the Gentiles may become [γένηται/*genētai*] acceptable', lies a reference to the initiating activity of God), and (2) they were 'clean' because they were *sanctified* by the Holy Spirit.

Paul did not think of his own ministry as involving literal cultic and priestly activity. But the concentration on sacrificial imagery is neither 'unintentional nor casual', as Dunn rightly observes. It is

---

7   ἱερουργέῳ/*hierourgeō* does not appear in the LXX or elsewhere in the New Testament. Philo and Josephus use the verb with reference to the offering of the first-fruits, spiritual burnt offerings and the sacrifice of investiture. The verb came to mean to 'perform the work of a priest', and then in a broad sense to 'present or offer sacrifices', without indicating whether or not a priest was responsible for the action. See C. Wiener, '*Ιερουργεῖν* (Röm 15:16)', *SPCIC* 2, 399-404, and G. Schrenk, *TDNT* 3, 251-252.

8   See Appendix B, 'What is "the offering of the Gentiles" (Rom 15:16)?'

9   J. D. G. Dunn, *Romans 9-16*, 860-861.

'Paul's way of underscoring his theological exposition of the gospel (1:16–15:13) in its outworking in his own missionary vocation'. In particular, this carefully chosen language 'brings home the continuity between his ministry and the whole revelation of Israel'. Yet even 'more striking' is the way Paul 'transforms and transcends all that had hitherto been bound up in that cultic language. By applying it to his own noncultic ministry of preaching the gospel he confirms that for him the cultic barrier between sacred and secular has been broken through and left behind'.[10]

The sacrificial language has been transformed—not simply 'spiritualised'—because of its eschatological fulfilment.[11] The 'day of salvation', the acceptable time (δεκτός/*dektos*, 2 Cor 6:2), has come and is present in the gospel which Paul the missionary proclaims. The goal of his activity, namely, 'that the offering of the Gentiles might become acceptable to God, sanctified by the Holy Spirit', is already being fulfilled and will be consummated on the final day.

We have thus seen that the apostle has used cultic language to describe the *goal* of his missionary task (v. 16). Two sentences later, when referring to what the risen Christ had accomplished through him, he expresses the *purpose* or *design* of these missionary endeavours in terms of Christ's lordship over the new people of God: '*for* the obedience (ὑπακοή/*hypakoē*) of the nations' (v. 18). The divine empowering and achievement in Paul's life had this specific aim in view and it was wholly in line with God's salvation historical purposes. This important expression is akin to and must be understood in the light of 'the obedience (ὑπακοή/*hypakoē*) of faith' which turns up in Romans 1:5 and 16:26, that is, at two highly significant positions in the letter, where it forms a frame or envelope (*inclusio*). The 'obedience of faith' in the introductory paragraph of 1:5 'serves to articulate the design of the apostle's missionary gospel' and is 'a programmatic statement of the main purpose of the letter to the Romans'[12] (see chapter 3). The totality

---

10   J. D. G. Dunn, *Romans 9-16*, 867.

11   Cf. W. Radl, 'Kult und Evangelium bei Paulus', *BZ* 31 (1987), 64–67.

12   D. Garlington, 'The Obedience of Faith in the Letter to the Romans. Part I: The Meaning of ὑπακοὴ πίστεως (Rom 1:5; 16:26)', *WTJ* 52 (1990), 201, and see his *'The Obedience of Faith'. A Pauline Phrase in Historical Context* (Tübingen: Mohr, 1991), 233–268, which follows N. T. Wright, 'The Messiah and the People of God. A Study in Pauline Theology with Particular Reference to the Argument of the Epistle to the Romans' (unpublished D. Phil. dissertation, Oxford, 1980), 175.

of Paul's missionary endeavours could be summed up by means of the three-fold phrase of Romans 1:5, 'for the obedience of faith (= purpose) among all the nations (= sphere) on behalf of his name (= ultimate focus)', while at 16:26, 'the obedience of faith' functions as part of the letter's concluding doxology in which the apostle praises God for his establishing the Roman Christians in the gospel preached by him.

This expression of the purpose of Paul's missionary labours, 'the obedience of the Gentiles', has been interpreted along two main lines:

(1) The *conversion* of the Gentiles. On this view, the 'obedience' of the nations is their 'coming to faith' or their 'acceptance of the gospel'.[13] Accordingly, Paul is asserting that the risen Christ, by his Spirit, has been mightily at work through his ministry for the purpose of bringing Gentiles to a saving faith. If, as many commentators suppose, the obedience of the Gentiles explains the expression in v. 16, 'the offering of the Gentiles', then this sacrifice is acceptable to God when they are converted, for it is then that they are brought into a new relationship with him through the preaching of the gospel.

(2) On the other hand, this obedience has been understood more broadly so as to include not only the Gentiles' *believing acceptance* of the gospel, but their *constancy* of Christian conduct as well. D. B. Garlington has recently argued from the wider context and the purpose of Romans for this interpretation of 'obedience' (ὑπακοή/*hypakoē*) in all three texts: Romans 1:5; 15:18; 16:26.[14] Accordingly, when Paul speaks of the goal for which the risen Christ has worked powerfully in his ministry as 'for (εἰς/*eis*) the obedience of the Gentiles' (v. 18), he 'envisages not only the believing reception of his gospel by the nations but also their constancy of Christian conduct'.[15]

The second view makes good sense in the light of (a) Paul's stated ambition of preaching the gospel where Christ has not been named (v. 20), which includes but is not limited to primary

---

13 So, for example, A. Schlatter, O. Michel, E. Käsemann, C. K. Barrett and C. E. B. Cranfield.

14 For his detailed arguments in relation to Rom 15:18, see D. B. Garlington, 'The Obedience of Faith', 207-223.

15 D. B. Garlington, 'The Obedience of Faith', 222.

evangelism,[16] and (b) the apostle's earnest desire that his converts will be found holy and blameless, and filled with the fruit of righteousness on the day of the Lord Jesus (Phil 1:9-11; Col 1:9-14, 22, 28; 1 Thess 3:12-13, etc.). In other words, Paul's great longing is for their full Christian maturity. He will be satisfied with nothing less.[17] Accordingly, when he speaks of 'the obedience of the Gentiles', he has in view not only their conversion, but also their growth in Christian maturity to full perfection.[18]

(c) How this missionary calling was being fulfilled (vv. 18-19).

In the very sentence where he spells out the purpose of his missionary activity in terms of winning obedience from the Gentiles (v. 18), Paul discloses the means by which this ministry was being fulfilled: he refers to 'what Christ has accomplished through me . . . by word and deed, by the power of signs and wonders, by the power of the Spirit of God' (vv. 18-19). The first expression, 'by word and deed', is as general in the Greek as it is in English and indicates that the risen Lord Jesus accomplished his purposes through Paul's spoken and written words, as well as his deeds, which included 'things done and suffered, conduct generally, the example set by his steadfast endurance, etc.'[19] This short description is then elaborated by two parallel phrases, 'by the power of signs and wonders' and 'by the power of the Spirit of God', which characterize that ministry 'as both powerfully confirmed and attested by accompanying miracles and also accomplished as a whole in the power of the Holy Spirit'.[20] The latter phrase which has reference to his total ministry indicates that as Christ worked effectively through him, so it was accomplished by means of the Spirit's enabling.

---

16   See below, pp. 42–45.

17   Akin to this is the notion of his converts being his hope, joy and crown, *if they stand fast* in the Lord (Phil 2:16; 1 Thess 2:19-20; cf. 2 Cor 11:2). Paul consistently lived his life in the light of the approaching day of Christ for on that occasion the final account of his stewardship, as evidenced in the lives of his converts, would be rendered. His readers' continued blamelessness and steadfastness, which would be the basis of his boast on that day, will demonstrate that his strenuous efforts for the gospel and for them will have been entirely fruitful.

18   Likewise, the 'offering of the Gentiles' (v. 16) has to do with the sacrifice presented to God on the final day—of which the collection may be regarded as an anticipation. Paul is speaking about the final goal of his ministry in both vv. 16 and 18.

19   C. E. B. Cranfield, *The Epistle to the Romans* 2 (Edinburgh: Clark, 1979), 759.

20   C. E. B. Cranfield, *Romans* 2, 759.

What then is the meaning of the first phrase, 'by the power of signs and wonders'? And what significance does it have in this description of Paul's ministry? 'Signs and wonders' (σήμεια καὶ τέρατα/*sēmeia kai terata*) is a rare combination in Paul's letters. It appears only three times and has negative connotations in its two other occurrences (2 Cor 12:12 and 2 Thess 2:9). Here, however, the apostle employs the expression positively in a way that seems designed to recall its OT equivalent.

'Signs and wonders' was a traditional way of speaking of the Exodus miracles (Exod 7:3, 9; 11:9-10; Deut 4:34; 6:22).[21] They are the events by which God redeemed his people from Egypt and brought them to the promised land.[22] The expression regularly designated events surrounding the great redemptive acts of God. 'Signs and wonders' were also associated in the OT with true prophecy (Isa 8:18; 20:3) and in the NT with the works of Jesus (cf. John 20:29-31; Acts 2:19, 22), together with the ministry of the apostles, including Paul, as well as some closely associated with them (Acts 2:43; 5:12; 14:3; 15:12; cf. Heb 2:3-4). Here in Romans 15:19 Paul is asserting that his ministry to the nations, through which Christ has effectively borne testimony,[23] stands within this salvation-historical framework. Indeed, his work as a missionary to the Gentiles (ἔθνη/*ethnē* appears three times in this context: vv. 16 [twice], 18) is itself one of those very redemptive acts of God. By mentioning 'signs and wonders' Paul is not simply affirming that, as God's special envoy to the nations, he has the *marks of a true apostle*, though this was undoubtedly correct—after

---

21 Note also Deut 7:19; 11:3; 26:8; 29:3; 34:11; Neh 9:10; Pss 78:43; 135:9; Jer 32:20-21; cf. Dan 4:2-3; 6:27; Acts 7:36. For further references see K. H. Rengstorf, *TDNT* 7, 200-269, F. Stolz, 'Zeichen und Wunder. Die prophetische Legitimation und ihre Geschichte', *ZTK* 69 (1972), 125-144, J. W. Woodhouse, 'Signs and Wonders in the Bible', in *Signs & Wonders and Evangelicals*, ed. R. Doyle (Homebush West, NSW: Lancer, 1987), 17-35, J. D. G. Dunn, *Romans 9-16*, 862-863, and D. A. Carson, 'The Purpose of Signs and Wonders in the New Testament', in *Power Religion. The Selling Out of the Evangelical Church?* ed. M. S. Horton (Chicago: Moody, 1992), 89-118.

22 So J. W. Woodhouse, in *Signs*, 22. After a survey of the biblical evidence for 'signs and wonders' he concludes: 'in the Bible the "significant wonders"—the wonders that matter for faith—are the events surrounding the great redemptive acts of God' (27). There are, of course, references to *rival* signs and wonders which are intended to lead people astray and 'will not call the people back to the historic redemptive acts of God' (28): Deut 13:1-3; Matt 24:24; Mark 13:22; 2 Thess 2:9-10; Rev 13:13-14.

23 Note especially Acts 14:3, where the Lord *confirms* the message of his grace by enabling Paul and Barnabas, who had spoken boldly on his behalf, 'to do miraculous *signs and wonders*'.

all, Christ had been working mightily through him. He is at the same time asserting that Christ's working through him is *part and parcel of God's redemptive activity*, associated with 'signs and wonders', which has been effected through Moses at the Exodus, the prophets, the saving ministry of Jesus and his apostles whose ministry was particularly to Jews. Paul's missionary calling and work *among the nations* stands within a salvation-historical framework, with which the purposes of God for the saving of both Jew and Gentile are closely bound, and that work was itself one of those very redemptive acts of God.

(d) The extraordinary results of Paul's work: he has fulfilled the gospel of Christ. (v. 19).

If the exalted Christ's working through his missionary led to a ministry that was powerfully carried out by means of word and deed, so that it could be said to have been accomplished in the power of the Spirit, then the *results* were no less extraordinary in terms of the extension of the work (v. 19b). Paul affirms that Christ's dynamic activity through him led to the result 'that (ὥστε/ *hōste*) from Jerusalem all the way around to Illyricum, I have fully proclaimed (πεπληρωκέναι/*peplērōkenai*) the gospel of Christ'. Consequently, he can say that 'there is no more place for me to work in these regions' (v. 23), and he now plans to visit Jerusalem, Rome and Spain.

Paul's claim seems to be incredible. It is perfectly understandable that, at this turning point in his ministry and before he moves to the west, he should feel a sense of fulfilment (cf. Acts 14:26). But to contend that he has *fulfilled* (or completed or fully preached) the gospel of Christ, and this in a broad arc from Jerusalem extending round to Illyricum, suggests that the apostle has 'gone over the top'! Several expressions urgently cry out for explanation if we are to make any sense of this claim. For instance, what does 'I have fulfilled/fully proclaimed (πεπληρωκέναι/*peplērōkenai*) the gospel of Christ' mean in the light of Paul's apparent qualifications of v. 20? How is the geographical frame of reference to be interpreted? Exegetes and theologians have made a number of suggestions in an attempt to make sense out of these words, and for the sake of convenience we shall examine the relevant phrases as follows:

1. The geographical reference: 'from Jerusalem all the way round to Illyricum'

The apostle saw a particular pattern in his missionary efforts which could be expressed within a geographical frame of reference. He has fulfilled the gospel 'from Jerusalem all the way round to Illyricum'.

The opening phrase 'from Jerusalem' is puzzling. Paul began his Christian preaching in Damascus and the surrounding area of Arabia (Acts 9:19-25), while his more extended work as a missionary to the Gentiles started when he was based in Antioch (Acts 13:1-3). We do not know of any important ministry in the Jerusalem area. Although he may have had an occasion in mind, such as his vision in the Temple relating to his call to preach to the Gentiles (Acts 22:19-21), or the time in Jerusalem when he was given the right hand of fellowship for his work among Gentiles (Gal 2:9), these are unlikely. In order to get round the difficulty both geographical references have been regarded as exclusive rather than inclusive (that is, 'not including Jerusalem or Illyricum'). Accordingly, it is taken to mean that he had preached from the boundary of Jerusalem to the boundary of Illyricum.[24] 'He is stating the limits of his preaching, so far, not claiming to have preached in both'.[25]

An alternative interpretation is to understand this reference within a salvation-historical perspective: Jerusalem was the starting point of the whole Christian mission (Luke 24:47; Acts 1:8, and Paul's strong emphasis on the priority of the Jew in hearing the gospel: cf. the 'first' in Rom 1:16, etc.), because it was from Jerusalem that the gospel went forth. U. Wilckens has suggested that, although Paul is the grammatical subject of the verb 'completed', the emphasis of the passage is so strongly placed on the effective working of Christ and his Spirit, that the logical subject in v. 19b is really the gospel itself (see below). Though Paul had not worked as a missionary in Jerusalem, he places it first in this

---

24　So E. Käsemann, *Commentary on Romans* (Grand Rapids: Eerdmans, 1980), 394, U. Wilckens, *Die Brief an die Römer 12-16* (Zürich: Benziger/Neukirchen: Neukirchener Verlag, 1982), 119-120, and A. J. Hultgren, *Paul's Gospel and Mission*, 131.

25　L. Morris, *The Epistle to the Romans* (Leicester: Inter-Varsity; 1988), 514. Cf. F. F. Bruce, *The Letter of Paul to the Romans* (London: Tyndale, 1963), 261, and D. Zeller, *Juden und Heiden in der Mission des Paulus* (Stuttgart: Katholisches Bibelwerk, 1976), 227, who argues that Paul is thinking of his own ministry, rather than more generally of the gospel's expansion (as in Col 1:5-6).

geographical sequence, for the gospel itself had begun in Jerusalem when it was preached there by the first apostles. The reference to Jerusalem, then, helps us to realize that Paul is not writing exclusively of his own work. Instead, he is setting it within the overlapping context of a universal gospel mission.[26] On this view which makes good sense in the context, behind Romans 15:19 stands a salvation-historical concept of mission.

Paul's description continues: 'and in a sweep round to Illyricum'. The words, 'in a sweep round' (κύκλῳ/*kyklō*, lit. 'in a circle'), are normally taken as referring to a broad arc or portion of a circle extending from Jerusalem to Illyricum.[27] We have no other evidence that Paul pushed as far north as Illyricum in his missionary work, but since the area did border on Macedonia it is just possible that he did. If, however, the preposition 'to' is used exclusively rather than inclusively and means 'up to' (rather than 'into'), then the phrase may simply be a reference to the northern limitation of Paul's Macedonian mission.[28] Illyricum would then signify the limit of the apostle's missionary endeavours. What does emerge from this geographical reference is that Paul's journeys were not 'sporadic, random skirmishes into gentile lands'[29] (cf. 2 Cor 1:17; 2:12).

2. A sense of completion: 'I have fulfilled the gospel of Christ'

Linked with the geographical frame of reference is Paul's amazing claim: 'I have fulfilled or completed the gospel of Christ'. He cannot mean that he has preached the gospel to every single

---

26 U. Wilckens, *Römer 12-16*, 120. Cf. E. Lohse, *TDNT* 7, 334, and G. Bornkamm, *Paul* (London: Hodder, 1969), 53. Similarly, W. P. Bowers, *Studies*, 20, comments, in relation to this first geographical reference, that the apostle was not describing his own missionary progress, i.e. his own chronological or geographical starting point 'but rather the proper originating point of every advance for the gospel in his day, because all missionary progress of the period was, both from a historical and from a theological point of view, necessarily "from Jerusalem"'.

27 Rather than a circle round about Jerusalem itself. So BAGD, 456–457, and most commentators.

28 One wonders whether Paul saw his work not simply as an arc but as the top half of a circle which presupposed that others were engaged in the lower half (through Egypt, Alexandria and North Africa). Cf. J. D. G. Dunn, *Romans 9-16*, 864. J. Knox, 'Romans 15:14-33 and Paul's Conception of his Apostolic Mission', *JBL* 83 (1964), 11, suggests that Paul may have hoped he might encircle 'the whole Mediterranean world' within his lifetime. Note A. J. Hultgren, *Paul's Gospel and Mission*, 132-133.

29 A. J. Hultgren, *Paul's Gospel and Mission*, 133.

person in these eastern regions or even to all the small towns and country districts of the lands he had evangelized.

The verb πληρόω/*pleroō*, which is used here, covers a wide range of meanings including 'to fill, make full, fulfil, complete or finish'.[30] On occasion, it carries the sense of 'doing something fully' or 'carrying it to completion'. So, for example, at Colossians 1:25 Paul writes about his divine commission to 'complete' the word of God, while in Acts 14:26 Luke records that Paul and Barnabas returned to Antioch, having 'completed' the work to which they had been called.[31] There is no exact parallel, however, to the idea of fulfilling 'the gospel'.

Paul frequently stresses the dynamic, almost personal, character of the gospel.[32] Here at Romans 15:19 εὐαγγέλιον/*euangelion* has this same dynamic connotation of the act of proclamation or the work of evangelism (note the parallel use of the cognate verb εὐαγγελίζομαι/*euangelizomai* at v. 20): Paul has completed 'the preaching of the gospel of Christ'. But in what sense has he done this? The following are some of the more significant views which have been presented:

a. An *eschatological* interpretation—the *fulfilment* of OT eschatology. An important body of scholarly opinion has suggested that here Paul was speaking about his having brought the gospel to its 'fulfilment', that is, to its destiny among the Gentiles.[33] Johannes Munck connected Romans 15:19 and Colossians 1:25 with 2 Timothy 4:17 ('that through me the message might be fully proclaimed, and that all the Gentiles might hear'), and related them all to the bringing in of 'the fulness of the Gentiles' in Romans 11:25. For Munck this was related to Paul's distinctive place in salvation history. He understood the apostle's call in terms of the Servant of Isaiah and Jeremiah, both of whom had significant ministries in relation to the Gentiles. So significant was the apostle's ministry that it was

---

30   BAGD, 670-672, and cf. G. Delling, *TDNT* 6, 286-298.

31   See also Acts 12:25 in relation to completing a mission of assistance, Col 4:17 of a ministry received in the Lord, and Luke 9:31 of the way of Jesus to the cross; cf. Acts 13:25; Rev 3:2. For further references see G. Delling, *TDNT* 6, 286-298.

32   Note the discussion of this important emphasis in chapter 5.

33   R. Asting, *Die Verkündigung des Wortes im Urchristentum* (Stuttgart: Kohlhammer, 1939), 138, was one of the first in recent times to suggest this line.

'more important than that of all the figures in Old Testament redemptive history, because he has been appointed by God to fill the key position in the last great drama of salvation'.[34]

The 'fulness of the Gentiles' was associated with an aim that consists in the hearing of the gospel by the Gentile world as a whole—at least representatively—and believing it. Paul's use of the cognate verb 'fulfil' (πληρόω/*pleroō*) in this context denotes that same fulness. So Munck puts it, 'From a purely territorial point of view, therefore, we can say that for the east the fullness of the Gentiles has been achieved'.[35] It still remains for Paul to preach Christ's gospel fully in the west.

Several recent writers, while not following all of Munck's conclusions, have tied this in with Paul's supposed conviction of the pressing imminence of the parousia, which leaves much too little time to take the gospel where it had not been heard before.[36] In general terms, however, Munck's eschatological interpretation of Paul's missionary calling has not convinced subsequent NT scholarship, while his particular treatment of Romans 15:19 has, by and large, been rejected. Munck rightly placed Paul's mission within an eschatological framework. Furthermore, many of his comments about the apostle's call being understood in terms of the Servant of Isaiah and Jeremiah are insightful.[37] But Munck's almost exclusively future orientation of the eschatological framework has been neglected, if not rejected outright, by the majority of recent writers. He emphasized in a profound way the 'not yet' in Paul's eschatological understanding of his mission, but the relevant texts in the apostle's letters stress the 'already' aspect of this tension. For Paul the most decisive event of the last days, viz. the death and resurrection of the Lord Jesus Christ, had already occurred and this was determinative for his own life and mission. His personal messianic encounter and commission on the Damascus road forced this recognition on him. Both his calling and his mission to be an apostle to the Gentiles were rooted in this Damascus christophany (which was itself bound up with the death and resurrection of Jesus), not in some future event.

---

34   J. Munck, *Paul and the Salvation of Mankind* (London: SCM, 1959), 43.
35   J. Munck, *Paul*, 301, cf. 47–52.
36   Note, for instance, C. K. Barrett, M. Black, E. Käsemann, H. Schlier and U. Wilckens.
37   See our treatment on pp. 6–7, 11–12.

Bowers thus correctly concludes:

> 'in his mission Paul was far more visibly and distinctly
> working from an eschatological event than towards one, [and]
> . . . while there is indeed a future aspect to his eschatological
> understanding of his mission, the dominant orientation is
> upon the 'already' rather than the 'not yet'.[38]

Finally and more specifically, the identification of the expression
'to fulfil of the gospel of Christ' (Rom 15:19) with 'the fulness of
the Gentiles' of Romans 11:25 has been criticized on exegetical
grounds.

To conclude: the eschatological interpretation of Romans 15:19
does not adequately explain the text within its immediate context,
nor does it come to grips with the dominant emphasis on the
'already' in Paul's understanding of his mission.

b.   The *dynamic preaching* of the gospel—the *manner* in which
Paul's mission was effected. J. H. Schütz[39] made the interesting
suggestion that 'fulfilling the gospel' describes not the finishing of
an assignment, but *the way in which Paul executed his task*: fully, in
word and deed, with signs and wonders, and in the power of the
Holy Spirit.   Paul set in motion forces by which Christ wins
obedience from the nations.

Certainly there is within this context the motif of an effective
and dynamic preaching of the gospel on the part of the apostle.
The gospel is fulfilled not simply when it is preached in the world,
but when it is dynamically and effectively proclaimed in the power
of the Spirit (cf. 1 Thess 1:5, 6) throughout the world, and
accepted in faith by men and women.   Like God's word of old (Isa
55:11) it is dynamic, achieving the very purpose for which it has
been sent forth.   Obviously this has particular reference to Gentiles,
since they are specifically mentioned in this context.

But there is some doubt as to whether this interpretation of the
manner in which Paul executed his task does justice to the
expression, 'to fulfil the gospel', which seems to suggest the
completing of an assignment.   Furthermore, in the immediate

---

38   W. P. Bowers, *Studies*, 149.
39   J. H. Schütz, *Paul and the Anatomy of Apostolic Authority* (Cambridge: Cambridge
     University Press, 1975), 46–47.

context Christ has so worked through the apostle that fulfilling the
gospel is presented as a result that has been achieved in line with
God's redemptive purposes. This element of completing a goal is
missing from Schütz's approach.

c. An *ecclesiastical* interpretation—the *scope* of Paul's mission. A
different understanding of our enigmatic phrase which draws
attention to the *scope* of Paul's mission is that of Paul Bowers.[40] He
examined a number of significant passages in the apostle's letters to
determine the kinds of activity that fell within the scope of Paul's
missionary calling. The first is primary evangelism. Whether the
apostle speaks of it in terms of the task assigned to him (1 Cor
1:17), his main line of action in a mission setting (Gal 4:13), or
what he would like to do in the future (2 Cor 10:16), he clearly
regarded primary evangelism as an important part of his mission.
That he 'perceives his role as initiatory in nature is apparent as well
in the specific metaphors he applies to his vocation',[41] namely,
planting (1 Cor 3:6-9; 9:7, 10, 11), laying foundations (Rom 15:20;
1 Cor 3:10), giving birth (1 Cor 4:15; Phlm 10) and betrothing (2
Cor 11:2).

But this is not all. Paul not only proclaimed the gospel and,
under God, converted men and women. He also founded churches
as a necessary element in his missionary task. Conversion to Christ
meant incorporation into him, and thus membership within a
Christian community. The apostle's letters are addressed to such
churches. Indeed, the existence of these congregations Paul regards
as an authentication of his apostleship (1 Cor 9:2; 2 Cor 3:1-3).[42]
From his *practice* of residential missions (at Corinth and Ephesus)
and nurture of churches (1 Thess 2:10-12), from his *priorities* (1
Thess 2:17–3:13; 2 Cor 2:12-13; 10:13-16), and from his *description
of his assignment* (Col 1:24–2:7; Rom 1:1-15; 15:14-16) in relation
to admonition and teaching believers to bring them to full maturity
in Christ, it is clear that *the nurture of emerging churches* is understood
by Paul to be 'an integral feature of his missionary task'.[43]

---

40 W. P. Bowers, 'Fulfilling the Gospel: The Scope of the Pauline Mission', *JETS* 30
     (1987), 185-198 (cf. also his *Studies*, 81-121). I am indebted to Bowers' insightful
     paper at this and a number of other points.
41 W. P. Bowers, 'Fulfilling the Gospel', 186.
42 W. P. Bowers, 'Fulfilling the Gospel', 187-188.
43 W. P. Bowers, 'Fulfilling the Gospel', 197; see especially 188-197.

Bowers takes the results of this inductive study back to Paul's statement of the overview of his mission in Romans 15:19-21, with his claim to have 'fulfilled the gospel', and asks, What sort of activity would Paul 'need to engage in order to arrive at this sense of accomplishment'? His response is: 'Paul's missionary vocation finds its sense of fulfilment in the presence of firmly established churches'.[44] Proclaiming the gospel meant for Paul not simply an initial preaching or with it the reaping of converts; it included also a whole range of nurturing and strengthening activities which led to the firm establishment of congregations. So, his claim to have 'fulfilled the gospel in an arc right up to Illyricum' signified that he had established strong churches in strategic centres of this area, such as Thessalonica, Corinth and Ephesus. Further evangelistic outreach and the upbuilding of congregations lay in the hands of others. But for the apostle there was no more place for him to work in these regions, and thus he was 'free' to go up to Jerusalem and move on to Spain via Rome.

Understanding Paul's enigmatic expression, 'I have fulfilled the gospel of Christ', in terms of the *scope* of his missionary activity which included (1) primary evangelism, (2) the nurture of emerging churches, and (3) their firm establishment as congregations, is correct, in my judgment. This suggestion fits neatly with the earlier conclusion that the purpose of Paul's labours, described as 'the obedience of the Gentiles', envisaged not only their conversion, but also their growth in Christian maturity to perfection.

(e) *Paul's all-consuming ambition: to preach Christ where he had not been named (vv. 20-21).*

In order to guard against any possible misunderstanding of his amazing claim to have 'fulfilled the gospel', Paul adds by way of qualification and explanation (v. 20) that his completing the gospel was only in accordance with his ambition to preach it where Christ had not been named, and not in an absolute sense. He has not fulfilled the gospel in every place between Jerusalem and Illyricum. As he speaks about his all-consuming ambition, Paul makes a very

---

44   W. P. Bowers, 'Fulfilling the Gospel', 198. A similar point had been made earlier by M. Kettunen, *Der Abfassungszweck des Römerbriefes* (Helsinki: Suomalainen Tiedeakatemin, 1979), 138; cf. A. J. M. Wedderburn, *The Reasons for Romans* (Edinburgh: Clark, 1988), 97.

important statement about his mission policy. He spells out 'a principal aspiration that guides the overall direction of his mission',[45] not a definitive law[46] or a restrictive canon of his apostolic commission. Paul is not prohibiting where he shall preach but selecting where he will make strategic choices to proclaim the gospel. In the original the negative is not linked to the verb 'proclaim' but to the adverb 'where': 'my ambition is to proclaim not where Christ has been named', that is, in the sense of acknowledged or worshipped.[47] Because Paul did not interpret his divine commission in a rigid or unimaginative way, there 'is no suggestion that he felt himself under an absolute obligation to refrain from ever visiting a church which had been founded by someone else'.[48] So, it was not inconsistent with these deep aspirations for him to pay the Christians in Rome a visit.

The purpose of Paul's ambition which guides the overall direction of his missionary activity is 'so as not to build on another's foundation' (v. 20b). By using the metaphor of a building he explains the preceding part of the verse and indicates to his readers that he wishes to go only where there is need for a foundation to be laid. Unfortunately, these words have often been read as indicating that he was simply a primary evangelist, only concerned with putting in the foundation where one was not already present. 1 Corinthians 3:5-15 with its imagery of a building (cf. v. 10, 'By the grace God has given me, I laid a foundation as an expert builder, and someone else is building on it'), is drawn in to support this notion of Paul as only a primary evangelist. But even if he makes it his practice not to build on another's foundation, he is still concerned about the kind of structure being erected on the foundation. After all, Paul does actually *build*! His letters themselves, as well as his practice, stated priorities and descriptions of his commission indicate, as we have already seen, his commitment to the upbuilding of congregations, not simply to

---

45   W. P. Bowers, 'Fulfilling the Gospel', 196, n. 24.

46   An 'unbroken rule' as the JB puts it.

47   Which is the significance of ὀνομάζομαι/*onomazomai* here (Eph 1:21; 2 Tim 2:19; cf. Josh 23:7; Esth 9:4; Isa 26:13).

48   C. E. B. Cranfield, *Romans* 2, 765; cf. N. A. Dahl, 'Missionary Theology', 75, W. P. Bowers, 'Fulfilling the Gospel', 196, n. 24. S. Pedersen, 'Theologische Überlegungen zur Isagogik des Römerbriefes', *ZNW* 76 (1985), 51-57, also rejects rigorist interpretations of Paul's 'work rule' of Rom 15:20, and shows how Paul has flexibly applied it at Corinth (cf. 2 Cor 10:12-18).

their founding—not only to their planting but also to their watering.[49]

His ambition to preach the gospel where Christ was not acknowledged as Lord, in order not to build on another's foundation (v. 20), is evidence that primary evangelism was *integral* to his missionary commission, although it was *not the only element* in that commission. Paul's work was not finished until he had instructed the Christians and left a mature and settled congregation.

Several significant points emerge from an examination of this stated ambition within its immediate context:

1. Paul's pioneer policy has the endorsement of OT Scripture

As he has frequently done in the Letter to the Romans, Paul turns once again to the OT Scriptures, this time in support of his pioneer policy of declaring the gospel where Christ has not been named (v. 21). A whole section of Isaiah has already served as a source of gospel *testimonia* in the letter; now Paul quotes from the fourth Servant Song (Isa 52:15 LXX) and refers to the effects of the Servant's ministry on many nations (ἔθνη/*ethnē*) and kings.

> 'Those who were not told about him will see, and those who have not heard will understand'.

This prophetic word endorsed the apostle's aim of making it his ambition to preach Christ in a *pioneer* situation, that is, where Gentiles had not been told about this Servant or his ministry on their behalf. The OT promise supported Paul's work of *primary* evangelism. He was to go to Gentiles who had *never heard*. He then found this word of God to be reliable for, as he pursued his ambition of preaching Christ where he was not known, people from many nations (ἔθνη/*ethnē*) in the eastern Mediterranean, began to *see* and to *understand* that the Servant's vicarious work of redemption was for them, and were converted.

---

49   1 Corinthians 3:6, 'I planted, Apollos watered', might be thought to contradict this and limit Paul's functions to initiatory action. However, as Bowers has rightly pointed out, Paul is stating 'not the terms of his commission but the actual historical experience of the Corinthian church in its earliest phase'; W. P. Bowers, 'Fulfilling the Gospel', 188, n. 9.

2. His work is a continuance of the Servant's ministry

In applying this OT text to his own missionary activity, Paul believed that he was carrying on the work of the Servant of Yahweh, even if he did not explicitly identify himself with this figure. We have already seen that he interpreted his missionary calling in terms of the Servant's commission (Gal 1:15-16; cf. Rom 1:1), and understood his role to be that of completing the Servant's task by taking the light of the gospel 'to the nations' (Isa 49:6). Here Paul's *pioneer policy* has OT endorsement in relation to the work of that same salvation historical figure.

3. Paul's pioneer ministry is consistent with the Lord's great compassion for the lost

In both the Isaianic passage and the context of Romans 15:21 the focus of attention is upon the needy recipients of this life-saving message—they are 'those who have not heard'. The OT paragraph underscores the great concern for the lost which lies at the heart of Yahweh himself, who out of compassion sends his Servant to meet this need. Paul's determined aim to preach Christ to Gentiles in a frontier situation not only has Scriptural endorsement but is also evidence of his deep-seated compassion for the lost. At the same time, it is at one with the Lord's kindness shown to needy Gentiles in his gracious redemptive plan.

Paul's profound concern for those who had not heard can be explained within the framework of God's grace and his own sense of obligation. We have already seen that he repeatedly and emphatically underscored the point that he was a surprising recipient of God's grace. He was totally undeserving of divine mercy; yet he received it and was given a lifetime ministry to men and women among the nations who were as lost as he once had been. His deep-seated compassion for them sprang out of his own profound sense of gratitude (cf. Rom 1:14).[50]

Conclusions

The aim of this second chapter, like the first, has been to determine what was distinctive about Paul's missionary activity. It is my contention that if by careful exegetical study we can arrive at some

---

50   See chapter 3.

understanding of these distinguishing marks, we will be less likely
to make quick or superficial applications from the apostle's ministry
or experience to our own lives and missionary strategies.

In Romans 15:14-21 Paul provides a brief overview of his
missionary career from its beginnings up to the time of writing the
letter, and he describes its amazing effects. His mission has been called
the theological corollary of his gospel exposition which has been
featured in the body of Romans. Paul knows that God's intention
from of old has been to save Gentiles. He has been given the
gospel for those Gentiles and his apostolic ministry is a significant
plank in the completion of that divine plan of salvation.

The following distinguishing marks of Paul's missionary activity
are delineated in this highly significant paragraph:

(1) Paul again stresses his total dependence on divine grace (cf.
Gal 1; Eph 3). The whole of his missionary career was due to the
grace of God. It was the source and power of his ministry.

(2) The apostle employs a cluster of OT priestly and cultic terms
that is quite amazing to describe the *content and goal* of his ministry.
The former is 'the *priestly duty* of proclaiming the gospel of God' (v.
16). He acts on Christ's behalf by discharging his priestly
responsibilities in relation to the cult itself, namely, the gospel of
God, while the *purpose* of his commissioning, and thus of his whole
missionary career, was 'so that the offering of the Gentiles might be
acceptable to God, sanctified by the Holy Spirit' (v. 16). This
unusual expression probably means that Paul presents *the Gentiles
themselves* as the offering. At the same time, in vv. 25-32 our
enigmatic phrase is expanded and given concrete expression by
reference to the collection for the saints. Accordingly, Paul's
liturgical language has a twofold perspective: the offering is the
Gentiles themselves and their material gifts brought to Jerusalem to
meet the economic needs of believers there.

But for all this, the apostle did not think of his own ministry as
involving literal cultic activity. The sacrificial language has been
transformed because of the eschatological fulfilment. The 'day of
salvation', the acceptable time (2 Cor 6:2), has come and is present
in the gospel which Paul the missionary proclaims. The goal of his
activity, namely, 'that the Gentiles might become an offering
acceptable to God, sanctified by the Holy Spirit', is already being
fulfilled and will be consummated on the final day.

(3) The goal of the Paul's missionary task which has been explained in cultic terms is further described in relation to Christ's lordship over the new people of God, that is, '*for* the obedience (ὑπακοή/*hypakoē*) of the nations' (v. 18). This important expression denotes not simply the conversion of the Gentiles or their coming to faith, but also their constancy in Christian conduct. Paul looks not only for the Gentiles' acceptance of the gospel, but for their growth in Christian maturity and perfection as well.

(4) The missionary endeavours of this apostle to the Gentiles were carried out by the risen Christ who worked powerfully through him, accomplishing his purposes by the Spirit's enabling. He was God's special envoy to the nations who had the marks of a true apostle. But the reference to 'signs and wonders' also shows that his missionary calling was *part and parcel of God's redemptive activity*. It stood within a salvation-historical context, with which the purposes of God for the saving of both Jew and Gentile were integrated, and was itself one of those redemptive acts.

(5) The results of Paul's work were extraordinary. In terms that might otherwise be dismissed as prophetic hyperbole, he affirms that Christ's dynamic activity through him led to the result 'that from Jerusalem all the way around to Illyricum, I have fulfilled the gospel of Christ' (v. 19). His journeys were purposeful, not 'sporadic, random skirmishes into gentile lands'. Further, his geographical reference suggests that his ministry fell within the overlapping context of a universal gospel mission—the gospel itself had begun in Jerusalem when it was preached there by the first apostles. His claim to have '*fulfilled* the gospel of Christ' is probably a reference to the scope of his missionary activity: it included primary evangelism, the nurture of Christians and the establishment of settled congregations. Paul is not suggesting that he had evangelized all the small towns and country districts of these eastern regions, much less that he had preached the gospel to every person there.

(6) Finally, Paul's completing the gospel in key centres of the eastern Mediterranean was consistent with his all-consuming passion of proclaiming the gospel where Christ had not been acknowledged or worshipped. This was Paul's ambition which guided the overall direction of his life. He did not wish to build on another's foundation for primary evangelism was *integral* to his missionary commission, although it was not the only element in

that commission. As we have seen, his work was not finished until he had instructed the Christians and left a mature and settled congregation.

Making it his aim to preach Christ in a *pioneer* situation was supported by the OT scriptures. Paul was continuing the work of the Servant of Lord (cf. Isa 52:15). He was to go to Gentiles who had never heard. And as he pursued this ambition of preaching Christ where he was not known, people from many nations in the eastern Mediterranean, began to *see* and to *understand* that the Servant's vicarious work of redemption was for them. Paul's deep-seated compassion for the lost was at one with the Lord's kindness shown to needy Gentiles in his gracious redemption plan.

Because these features were distinctive to Paul's missionary activity, we ought not to apply them directly to the endeavours of contemporary missionaries. However, even in this highly significant paragraph which focusses on the distinguishing marks of Paul's missionary calling and ministry, there are hints of a wider teaching on mission, a broadening out, so to speak. Three points are worth noting:

(a) *The grace of God.* No one would suggest, least of all Paul himself, that the grace of God which he experienced in such abundant measure was limited to his ministry. Otherwise it ceases to be grace. Instead, the inference may be drawn that those who understand something of God's purposes to save men and women, and who proclaim the gospel to the lost may also experience the grace of God as the source and power of their ministry.

(b) *Paul's missionary work as part of a larger whole.* It is significant that, in a paragraph which focusses on Pauline distinctives, his missionary activity is viewed as *part of a larger whole.* Paul knew that he played an important role in the redemptive plan of God. At the same time, he recognized that others were also labouring in accordance with the divine purposes (cf. Rom 15:18-20). Other Christian workers held the gospel in common with him and they were laying the same foundation that he laid, namely, Jesus Christ. This is inferred in v. 18 and made explicit in v. 20, where Paul asserts that he goes to pioneer situations because he does not wish to 'build on someone else's foundation'. The purposes of God included the apostle to the Gentiles within their focus, but these purposes were broader than Paul himself. It will be necessary to take this issue up in the next chapter. For the moment, however, we note it in this significant context.

(c) *Concern for the lost.* Our study of Romans 15 has shown that Paul's great longing for those who had never heard of God's Servant and his saving work was not unique. His deep-seated concern, which found expression in his pioneer missionary endeavours, was consistent with the kindness and compassion of the Lord himself who sent his Servant to the Gentiles. Paul was *consumed by* a *passion* which mirrored the character of the Lord himself. If our lives mirror his character, then we too should be consumed by passion for the lost of our generation.

Appendix B. What Is 'the Offering of the Gentiles' (Rom 15:16)?

It is not entirely clear as to what is meant by the expression 'the offering of the Gentiles'.[51] (1) Most commentators take Paul's statement to mean that he presents *the Gentiles themselves as the offering* which is acceptable to God.[52]

(2) As a modification of this it has been suggested that the Gentiles themselves are the offering, but in vv. 25-32 our enigmatic phrase is expanded and given concrete expression with reference to the collection for the saints. Accordingly, Paul's liturgical language has two perspectives: the offering which is the Gentiles themselves

---

51   προσφορά/*prosphora* could refer to 1. the act of 'bringing' or 'presenting' an offering, both literally and figuratively (Heb 10:10, 14, 18; Acts 24:17; 1 *Clem* 40:4) and, as here, 2. 'that which is brought', 'gift', 'offering', again both figuratively and literally (Acts 21:26; Eph 5:2; Heb 10:5, 8; cf. Sir 14:11; 34:18; 1 *Clem* 36:1). Cf. BAGD, 720, and K. Weiss, *TDNT* 9, 68.

52   The genitive 'of the Gentiles' is treated as a genitive of apposition and the phrase understood epexegetically, 'the offering *which is* the Gentiles'. Cf. H. A. W. Meyer, *Critical and Exegetical Handbook to the Epistle to the Romans* 2 (Edinburgh: T. & T. Clark, ²1876), 345, 'The Gentiles converted, and through the Spirit consecrated as God's property, are the offering which Paul, as the priest of Jesus Christ, has brought to God'. R. Dabelstein, *Die Beurteilung der "Heiden" bei Paulus* (Frankfurt/Bern: Lang, 1981), 112, comments that 'the obedience of the Gentiles' in v. 18 explains what this 'offering of the Gentiles' signifies, while M. Hengel, 'Origins of the Christian Mission', 51, regards the Gentiles themselves as the sacrifice who by being won are brought to

and their concrete material gifts brought to Jerusalem to meet the economic needs of believers there.[53]

(3) As a variation on the majority opinion, 'the offering' which Paul presents is interpreted in terms of 'the whole of the Gentile world' itself. The real difficulty with this view, however, is that the offering is said to be 'sanctified by the Holy Spirit', a predicate which refers to Christians, i.e. *believing* Gentiles.[54]

(4) A strong minority case has been made in favour of taking this phrase as 'the offering *made by* the Gentiles'. On this view the worshippers are the Gentiles, with Paul's responsibility as the priest being to ensure that their offering is presentable according to the requirements of the cult. 'It is in his preaching and expounding that Paul offers them up'.

On balance, we prefer (2)—the offering is the Gentiles themselves, epitomized by the material gifts brought by their representatives to meet the needs of the Jerusalem believers.

---

their 'full number' (Rom 11:25). He also understands this as connected 'with the praise to God offered by believing Gentiles' in vv. 9-13.

53   S. Pedersen, 'Theologische Überlegungen', 47-67.

54   So E. Käsemann, *Romans*, 392-393, consistent with his thoroughgoing apocalyptic interpretation of Pauline thought, claims that the apostle is 'here calling himself the priest of the Messiah Jesus to *the whole of the Gentile world* (our italics)'. For a criticism and modification of this see A. J. Hultgren, *Paul's Gospel and Mission*, 134-135.

CHAPTER 3

THE LOGIC OF PAUL'S GOSPEL

Romans 1:1-17

As might be expected in the first two chapters, where we examined those passages that speak of Paul's calling to be an apostle and the amazing results of his missionary endeavours, the focus of attention has been upon the distinctives of his mission and its role within divine salvation history. Paul's being set apart by God before he was born, the personal revelation of Christ in him on the Damascus road, his commission to go to the Gentiles which echoes OT calling narratives, and his place within the *mystery* of God were just some of the special features we observed in chapter 1. Likewise, important distinguishing marks of Paul's missionary career were delineated in our second chapter as we looked at the amazing success of his mission. These included his all-consuming ambition of proclaiming Christ in pioneer situations, the goals of his mission and its content, as well as his statements about the ascended Christ's mighty working through him by the power of the Holy Spirit. In both of these chapters we sought to find out as much as we could about Paul's understanding of *his* own mission. This attempt to analyze the theology of *his* mission was part of a broader enquiry into his *theology of mission* generally.

As we now turn more directly to this wider issue we run into a complex problem. It is this: although the apostle makes a number of important statements in his letters about his own missionary calling and its place within God's purposes, he does not seem, at first glance, to say a great deal about how the Christians in his congregations were to carry on his work or to be caught up with his mission and so be involved in these saving purposes of God. What are we to make of these omissions?

How did Paul understand his missionary activity in relation to that of others? What are the links, if any, between his own dynamic endeavours and that of his fellow believers? He is certainly aware and approves of the work which other Christians are doing (cf. Rom 15:18-21). But what is his understanding of their activity in relation to his own? How are we to explain this peculiar situation with Paul, who at every turn is preoccupied with an active mission to the Gentiles, failing clearly to indicate independent responsibility in such a mission for his churches?[1] A related question which we shall take up in detail later on, also demands an answer: why is so little written in the Pauline letters about the need for Christians to evangelize?

These issues are both important and complex. They have often puzzled Christians and cry out for answers. As a first step in addressing them we return to Paul's commissioning passages and his overview of Romans 15 since they provide us with a number of significant clues. Perhaps surprisingly, in these highly personalized paragraphs (and we have looked at only three of them: Gal 1:11-17; Eph 3:1-13; Rom 15:14-21), where the distinctives of his apostleship are to the fore, Paul makes it plain that his special missionary activity was *part of a larger whole* (see chapter 2). It was set within an eschatological frame of reference, namely, the 'divinely superintended ingathering of the nations of OT expectation'[2] and intimately bound up with the ongoing advance of the gospel of God. But the ingathering of the nations was vaster than Paul's own contribution, however brilliant this might have been, while the dynamic march of the gospel throughout the Mediterranean world was broader than Paul's own proclamation of the kerygma, since other Christians were caught up in it.

In gathering together these clues we note that in Galatians 1, although the means by which the gospel came to Paul was distinctive, namely, via a christophany, its content (Jesus Christ, the Son of God), scope and ongoing achievements were not limited to

---

1   D. Zeller, 'Theologie der Mission bei Paulus', in *Mission im Neuen Testament*, ed. K. Kertelge (Freiburg/Basel/Wien: Herder, 1982), 164, claims that while Paul develops a theological understanding of his own mission, he does not expand upon that of other missionaries or other church situations.

2   W. P. Bowers, *Studies*, 172. See also my article, 'Paul's Missionary Calling within the Purposes of God', in *In the Fullness of Time: Biblical Studies in Honour of Archbishop Donald Robinson*, ed. D. Peterson and J. Pryor (Homebush West, NSW: Lancer, 1992), 131-148.

him. Indeed, the very fact that he was commissioned to proclaim this saving message among the Gentiles (v. 16), establishes the point. In the redemptive plan of God it was through the gospel, namely, the placarding of Jesus Christ as crucified, that the Father was drawing men and women to himself and into a living relationship with his Son, the Lord Jesus. That gospel was identified with the covenant promises made to Abraham (Gal 3:8) and as Paul, or others, preached it, so the promised blessings were extended to Gentiles. Similar points could be made in relation to the *mystery* of Ephesians 3. The Pauline gospel had a world-wide missionary horizon from the beginning, and other Christians, besides Paul, were caught up in its proclamation.

Further, it is obvious that while the 'gospel of the Lord Jesus Christ' lay at the heart of all that Paul did, as the divine message it was making its triumphal progress *throughout the world*—that is, where Paul was at work *and beyond*. The 'gospel' had already done this in Rome (cf. Rom 1:8)—it had reached the capital before Paul's letter, and it was growing and bearing fruit at Colossae where Epaphras had evangelized (Col 1:6). Its content focussed on the risen and exalted Lord Jesus and, because it was intimately related to God's saving purposes, it could not in the nature of the case be restricted simply to what Paul did.

In the light of this initial evidence from passages that deal particularly with Paul's missionary apostleship, we believe that it is the gospel of the Lord Jesus Christ within God's purposes which serves as *the bridge between Paul's own missionary activity and that of others*. The apostolic kerygma appears to be the *critical link* between the two, and thus potentially provides the connection between Paul's teaching about his own mission and that of mission generally.

In an attempt, then, to furnish a proper basis for a statement on Paul's theology of mission, and to justify our claim that the 'gospel' provides the connection between his activity and that of other Christians, we intend to look specifically at two related issues concerning this motif of the gospel in Romans 1:1-17. The first is Paul's own involvement in the gospel. The relationship of apostle and gospel is a major theme of the epistle; it is mentioned in the first verse (1:1) and runs like a scarlet thread throughout to the fifteenth chapter (vv. 19-20) and the concluding doxology (16:25-27). Secondly, we shall attempt to expound what Romans 1 says about the gospel in God's saving purposes. From this two-fold analysis a number of important conclusions regarding 'the logic of Paul's gospel' will emerge.

Paul's Involvement in the Gospel

[1] Paul, a servant of Christ Jesus, called to be an apostle and set apart for the gospel of God— [2] the gospel he promised beforehand through his prophets in the Holy Scriptures [3] regarding his Son, who as to his human nature was a descendant of David, [4] and who through the Spirit of holiness was declared with power to be the Son of God by his resurrection from the dead: Jesus Christ our Lord. [5] Through him and for his name's sake, we received grace and apostleship to call people from among all the Gentiles to the obedience that comes from faith. [6] And you also are among those who are called to belong to Jesus Christ.

[7] To all in Rome who are loved by God and called to be saints: Grace and peace to you from God our Father and from the Lord Jesus Christ.

[8] First, I thank my God through Jesus Christ for all of you, because your faith is being reported all over the world. [9] God, whom I serve with my whole heart in preaching the gospel of his Son, is my witness how constantly I remember you [10] in my prayers at all times; and I pray that now at last by God's will the way may be opened for me to come to you. [11] I long to see you so that I may impart to you some spiritual gift to make you strong— [12] that is, that you and I may be mutually encouraged by each other's faith. [13] I do not want you to be unaware, brothers, that I planned many times to come to you (but have been prevented from doing so until now) in order that I might have a harvest among you, just as I have had among the other Gentiles. [14] I am obligated both to Greeks and Non-Greeks, both to the wise and the foolish. [15] That is why I am so eager to preach the gospel also to you who are at Rome.

[16] I am not ashamed of the gospel, because it is the power of God for the salvation of everyone who believes: first for the Jew, then for the Gentile. [17] For in the gospel a righteousness from God is revealed, a righteousness that is by faith from first to last, just as it is written: 'The righteous will live by faith'.

Because of limitations of space we shall restrict our examination of Paul's involvement in the gospel to the epistolary opening of Romans 1:1-17.

It has recently been claimed that, while christology is the *theological ground and starting point* of Romans, that is, the theological focus, and salvation history the *theological framework* within which Paul expresses his main ideas in Romans, the 'gospel' is the *theme* of the letter. The noun 'gospel' and its cognate verb are prominent in the introduction (1:1, 2, 9, 15) and conclusion (15:16, 19, 20; cf. also 16:25) of the epistle, that is, its epistolary frame. Also, the gospel has 'pride of place' in Paul's thematic statement of 1:16-17.[3] Although the topics of 'salvation' and 'justification by faith' are often singled out and made the key to Paul's epistle, both are subordinate to the gospel. Further, a topic as broad as 'gospel' is needed to include the various materials in the letter.[4]

(a) Set apart for the gospel of God (v. 1).

The opening verse of Romans draws attention to Paul's involvement in the gospel. Here he introduces himself as 'a servant of Jesus Christ, called to be an apostle, *set apart for the gospel of God*'[5]. We have already seen that Paul was separated at his conversion and commissioning on the Damascus road and his task was to serve the gospel (cf. Gal 1:15-16 with its echo of Isa 49:1; Jer 1:5). If one is speaking about the *eschatological basis* of Paul's separation, then it was grounded in a *past* event, the personal revelation of the resurrected and exalted Lord Jesus to him, rather than a future one, such as an imminent parousia.

As one who is set apart[6] for the gospel Paul is called to preach it. He serves the gospel 'by an authoritative and normative proclamation of it'.[7] Paul was wholly committed to the gospel.

---

3   D. Moo, *Romans 1-8* (Chicago: Moody, 1991), 28.

4   D. Moo, *Romans 1-8*, 28. Cf. 59-74, esp. 73-74.

5   The Greek is ἀφωρισμένος εἰς εὐαγγέλιον θεοῦ/*aphōrismenos eis euangelion theou*.

6   In using the verb 'set apart' (ἀφορίζω/*aphorizō*) Paul may well have had in mind a passage such as Leviticus 20:26, 'You shall be holy to me; for I the Lord am holy, and separated you from the other peoples to be mine' (cf. Exod 13:12), where the two notions of holiness and consecration are in view. And, 'the turn of the ages effected by Christ meant that the ideal of separation *from* the Gentiles now became for Paul separation *for the sake of* the Gentiles', J. D. G. Dunn, *Romans 1-8*, 9; cf. O. Haas, *Paulus*, 8-9.

7   C. E. B. Cranfield, *Romans 1*, 53.

From the time of his conversion onwards it was the dominant and determinative focus of his whole life. D. Moo rightly observes: 'Paul is claiming that his life is totally dedicated to God's act of salvation in Christ—a dedication that involves both his own belief in, and obedience to, that message as well as his apostolic proclamation of it'.[8] 'Gospel' (εὐαγγέλιον/*euangelion*) here has a verbal nuance to it (as a noun of agency): it is the *act of preaching the gospel* that is in view. However, this is not all that is implied by the term, for the following relative clause draws attention to its content, namely, that 'which God promised beforehand through his prophets in the holy scriptures' (v. 2). 'The content of the message and its proclamation are not two distinct meanings of the word εὐαγγέλιον [*euangelion*], only two sides of one concept'.[9]

(b) The goal of this missionary gospel (v. 5).

Through the mediation of the risen and glorified Lord Jesus Paul has received his apostolic commission (lit. 'grace and apostleship') and, in what has been claimed as 'a programmatic statement of the main purpose of the letter to the Romans',[10] he speaks of the goal of that missionary commission as: 'to bring about the obedience of faith among all the Gentiles[11] for the sake of the name of Christ'. The three prepositional phrases in this statement, which denote *purpose* ('for the obedience of faith'), *sphere* ('among all the Gentiles') and *ultimate focus* ('for the sake of his name'), epitomize 'the totality of Paul's missionary endeavors'.[12]

This expression, 'the obedience of faith (εἰς ὑπακοὴν πίστεως/*eis hypakoēn pisteōs*)', must be of considerable importance for it appears again at 16:26 as part of the letter's concluding

---

8   D. Moo, *Romans 1-8*, 37.

9   E. Molland, *Das paulinische Euangelion. Das Wort und die Sache* (Oslo: Dybwad, 1934), 48. Cf. J. H. Schütz, *Paul*, 40. On the background to Paul's use of εὐαγγέλιον/*euangelion*, see Appendix C.

10 D. B. Garlington, 'The Obedience of Faith', 201, and his *'The Obedience of Faith'*, 233-253, which follow N. T. Wright, 'The Messiah', 175.

11 On the question as to whether ἔθνη/*ethnē* means 'Gentiles' or 'nations' see D. Moo, *Romans 1-8*, 49-50.

12 D. B. Garlington, 'The Obedience', 203. The close juxtaposition between apostle and gospel in this context (as often elsewhere in Paul) supports the idea that the goal of his apostleship is also the purpose of his missionary gospel. His separation as an apostle 'for the gospel of God' (v. 1) is amplified in these words of v. 5: 'for the obedience of faith among all the Gentiles'.

doxology, and thus forms an *inclusio* with 1:5.[13] Garlington argues, in the light of these two important references at the beginning and end of the letter, that:

> 'the obedience of faith' is to be regarded as a phrase of some significance for the understanding of Paul. It is, in other words, *his own articulation of the design and purpose of his missionary labors:* God is now bringing his purposes to pass in salvation history through Paul's gospel, i.e., the preaching of Jesus Christ [16:25]. Paul's commission then is to be viewed as nothing less than the eschatological actualization of the eternal plan to create faith's obedience among the nations.[14]

The precise meaning of the phrase (as distinct from its function), which is unique to the whole of pre-Christian literature and even to Paul himself, has been disputed. Many commentators regard faith and obedience as equivalents.[15] However, while there is undoubtedly a close relationship between the two concepts, with similar assertions being made about each in Romans,[16] they are not identical. Perhaps the best rendering of the original is 'faith's obedience' (or 'believing obedience'; with 'of faith' [πίστεως/ *pisteōs*] being an adjectival genitive). This preserves the apparently deliberate ambiguity of the original that denotes 'an obedience which consists in faith and an obedience which finds its source in faith'.[17]

But even if there is some doubt about the exact nuance of Paul's expression, the immediate context of Romans 1:5,[18] the flow of the

---

13   In both references 'the obedience of faith' is an eschatological reality: it stands in direct relation to 'the prophetic scriptures' and such a response by Gentiles is the purpose for which the revelation of the mystery looked (16:25-26). Note the discussion in chapter 2 of Romans 15:18 where the goal of Paul's calling as a missionary is spelled out in terms of the closely related notion: '*for* the obedience of the Gentiles'.

14   D. B. Garlington, 'The Obedience', 205 (his italics).

15   So that 'of faith' (πίστεως/*pisteōs*) is treated as a genitive of apposition. Commentators who make the identification between the two nouns include C. K. Barrett, J. Calvin, C. E. B. Cranfield, E. Käsemann, J. Murray, H. Ridderbos, W. Sanday and A. C. Headlam, H. Schlier and U. Wilckens.

16   Rom 1:8 with 16:19; 10:16a with 16b; 11:23 with 30, 31; 1:5 with 15:18.

17   D. Garlington, 'The Obedience', 224.

18   Paul includes the Roman Christians in 1:6 within the scope of his apostolic commission to promote 'the obedience of faith' (and they were already believers). His earnest desire to impart some spiritual gift so that his and their *faith* might be mutually strengthened (vv. 11, 12) can only be understood of the advance of those already committed to Christ, while the 'harvest' he wishes to reap among them probably has to do with their progress in the faith as well as the conversion of other Gentiles in the surrounding area (see below). Similarly, his obligation and eagerness to preach the gospel in Rome (vv. 14, 15) seems to mean more than the conversion of non-Christians to the faith.

argument in chapters 1-8,[19] together with other instances in Paul's letters of the language of obedience which refer to Christian behaviour, all indicate that the apostle has in view the believer's total response to the gospel, not simply his or her initial conversion. The phrase 'captures the full dimension of Paul's apostolic task, a task that was not confined to initial evangelization but that included also the building up and firm establishment of churches'.[20]

This notion of a total response accords well with the conclusions already reached in relation to the parallel expression of 15:18, 'the obedience of the Gentiles', which focusses not simply on the nations coming to faith or their acceptance of the gospel, but on their initial response *and* constancy in Christian conduct as well.

(c) Serving God wholeheartedly in the gospel of his Son (v. 9).

Paul's *total* involvement in the gospel of God's Son is to the fore in his third reference to the significant term εὐαγγέλιον/*euangelion*, for here he makes an important statement about his rendering spiritual service in its proclamation. After a long salutation (vv. 1-7), the apostle begins his thanksgiving paragraph by assuring his readers that he gave thanks to God for their faith which was proclaimed far and wide (v. 8). He then introduces an oath (v. 9), following which he appears to interrupt his apology for not having already visited the Roman Christians, and maintains the thrust of the opening paragraph with its references to his missionary commission and gospel: '[God] whom I serve with my spirit in the gospel of his Son'.

Using a verb, 'I serve' (λατρεύω/*latreuō*), that was employed exclusively of religious service in the LXX[21] and was determinative of the NT occurrences where it has no reference to human relations, Paul speaks of his active service to God. This was a total

---

19   Where Paul's discussion of justification by faith is followed by the demand that those who are righteous before God pursue righteousness of life and sanctification.

20   D. Moo, *Romans 1-8*, 45.

21   Either to Israel's God or to the gods of the nations. It could describe the cultic service of Israel as a whole, and on occasion conveyed 'the idea of fidelity and devotion to God as lord and master in the broadest possible terms' (D. G. Peterson, *Engaging with God. A biblical theology of worship* (Leicester: IVP, Apollos, 1992), 179-180; cf. Deut 10:12-13; Josh 24:14-24). However, the terminology was mostly applied in the specific sense of honouring God by ritual observance (Cf. Exod 3:12; 2 Sam 15:8).

involvement of his whole person ('in my spirit'),[22] and the sphere of his ministry was 'in the gospel of his Son'. Here εὐαγγέλιον/ *euangelion* is used in an active sense (a noun of agency), meaning 'the proclamation of the gospel' rather than its content, and it is equivalent to the verb εὐαγγελίζομαι/*euangelizomai* ('to preach the gospel'). Paul puts his whole person into proclaiming the gospel of God's Son.

Perhaps in deliberate contrast to the typically cultic worship of the Jews this missionary states that he has given his life to the service of God in the preaching of the gospel. His ongoing proclamation was 'a religious act comparable with the praise offered in conjunction with the sacrificial ritual of the tabernacle or temple . . . it is clear from what follows in the context that *gospel preaching* was the focus and goal of all his activity (cf. 1:11-15)'.[23]

(d) Eager to preach the gospel in Rome (v. 15).

At the conclusion of the introductory thanksgiving paragraph and immediately prior to his highly-charged, thematic statement about the *gospel* (vv. 16-17), Paul speaks of his great eagerness to preach it in Rome. He knows that he is a debtor to all the Gentiles. In a solemn affirmation he states that he is *under obligation* to those who are 'barbarians' no less than to those who are 'Greeks', to the wise as well as to the foolish (v. 14). In fact, Paul was obligated to Christ who had died for him. But a debt to Christ was transformed 'into a debt to those whom Christ wished to bring to salvation'. Thus, 'obligation to him who died produces obligation to those for whom he died'.[24] Paul's readiness to preach the gospel knew no limits. His desire to come to Rome was not just a question of his personal inclination. It was a consequence of his obligation to God.

However, Paul's eagerness was not simply to preach the gospel *in the city* of Rome and its environs, where there were undoubtedly many non-Christians. His precise wording is '*to*[25] *you also* who are

---

22   This is not a reference to the Holy Spirit as such, but to Paul's own spirit (which, of course, had been renewed and empowered by the Holy Spirit): the phrase signifies with his 'whole person'.

23   D. G. Peterson, *Engaging with God*, 180.

24   P. Minear, 'Gratitude and Mission in the Epistle to the Romans', in *The Obedience of Faith* (London: SCM, 1971), 102-110, esp. 104.

25   Greek: καὶ ὑμῖν/*kai humin*. It could be 'among you' if the preposition ἐν/*en* is taken as original. But even this does not alleviate the problem for the expression has to do with results within the Christian community whatever else it may imply in relation to the general population in the capital.

in Rome', that is, *to the recipients* of the letter who have already been described as believers (cf. v. 8, 'your faith is proclaimed in all the world'). In what sense, then, does he 'preach the gospel' to Christians?

A correct answer to this question can be obtained only by determining how Paul uses 'gospel' terminology elsewhere in his letters as well as in the immediate context of Romans 1. The following points are pertinent:

(1) Here in v. 15, where the verb εὐαγγελίζομαι/*euangelizomai* appears, it is the proclamation of the gospel that is in view, rather than some general activity of preaching.[26] This is made clear in the immediately following words (v. 16) where Paul explains the reason for his eagerness: '*for* I am not ashamed of the gospel (εὐαγγέλιον/*euangelion*)'. Also, Paul's normal usage of the verb εὐαγγελίζομαι/*euangelizomai* is against the general meaning of 'preach'. This verb which focusses on 'the central missionary nature of [his] apostolic activity' is used by the apostle twenty one times.[27] Often it is employed specifically with 'gospel' as its object (1 Cor 15:1; 2 Cor 11:7; Gal 1:11). But even in those contexts where the cognate noun is not present, the notion of proclaiming the gospel is in view (cf. Rom 10:15 with v. 16; 2 Cor 10:16; Gal 4:13; 1:8; and Rom 15:20 in the light of v. 19). Paul knows that he has been sent by Christ *to preach the gospel* (1 Cor 1:17; 9:16-18). One may conclude that 'in almost every instance the verb εὐαγγελίζεσθαι [*euangelizesthai*] seems to presuppose the definition of its cognate noun'.[28] On grounds of both context and Pauline usage the verb here in Romans 1:15 means to 'preach the gospel', not to 'proclaim' or 'preach' in a general sense.

(2) Although this verb εὐαγγελίζομαι/*euangelizomai* ('to preach the gospel') is often taken to refer only to initial or primary evangelism, Paul employs the word-group to cover the whole range of evangelistic and teaching ministry—from the initial proclamation

---

26   N. Turner, *Grammatical Insights into the New Testament* (Edinburgh: Clark, 1965), 92, disposes of the problem by understanding the verb as 'tell', and takes the text to mean: 'I am anxious to tell you in Rome also my own point of view'. But as L. Morris, *Romans*, 65, n. 155, rightly observes, this is 'an unnatural meaning for the verb as Paul uses it' and it does not fit the context, particularly the explanatory clause in v. 16 with its use of εὐαγγέλιον/*euangelion*.

27   J. H. Schütz, *Paul*, 39. Rom 1:15; 10:15; 15:20; 1 Cor 1:17; 9:16 (twice), 18:15:1, 2; 2 Cor 10:16; 11:7; Gal 1:8 (twice), 9, 11, 16, 23; 4:13; Eph 2:17; 3:8; 1 Thess 3:6.

28   J. H. Schütz, *Paul*, 39. Note also his treatment of Gal 1:9, 16, 23 and 1 Thess 3:6.

of the gospel to the building up of believers and grounding them firmly in the faith. On occasion, when the apostle harks back to his own preaching of the kerygma in the founding of churches, an evangelizing activity which aims at conversions is specially in mind (cf. 1 Cor 4:15). But Paul did not understand his apostolic separation for the gospel (Rom 1:1; cf. 1 Cor 1:17) or his service in the gospel (Rom 1:9) solely in terms of its initial proclamation. The gospel is not simply 'the initial impulse on the way to salvation'.[29] It is the message by which men and women are finally saved. The Christian life is certainly created through the gospel (1 Cor 4:15; Col 1:5-6); but it is also lived in the sphere of this dynamic and authoritative message (cf. Phil 1:27). It needs therefore to be preached to those who have already received it and have become Christians. Believers do not leave the gospel behind or progress beyond it as they grow and mature in their faith. They stand fast in this kerygma and are being saved through it if they hold firmly to it (1 Cor 15:1-2), for it is in this authoritative announcement that true hope is held out to them (Col 1:5, 23).

(3) A similar usage in support of a wide-ranging series of activities being subsumed under the notion of preaching the gospel, occurs in Ephesians 3:8 where God's grace given to Paul consisted in his 'bringing the Gentiles the good news (εὐαγγελίσασθαι/ *euangelisasthai*)[30] of Christ's unfathomable wealth'. In the present context the object of the verb to 'bring the good news' is 'the unsearchable riches of Christ'. This expression is wide-ranging and suggests that the apostle's commission involved the presentation of an authoritative message that was both glorious and infinite. It is difficult to envisage how Paul or his colleagues could present to Gentiles this 'good news of Christ's unfathomable wealth' in a brief or summary fashion. This comprehensive phrase suggests that time for careful teaching, instruction and application was called for—that is, something more than is suggested by initial evangelism—if the content of these riches in Christ were to be understood and appropriated by the Gentiles for whom they were intended.

---

29 J. D. G. Dunn, *Romans 1-8*, 34, against D. Zeller, *Juden*, 55-58, who thinks that the range of activities covered by this verb is narrowly fixed.

30 Neither the aorist tense of the verb (εὐαγγελίσασθαι/*euangelisasthai*) nor the clause as a whole suggests that the apostle is here referring simply to primary evangelism. If any significance attaches to the tense at all, it is that an aorist was appropriate when summing up the content of his commission.

(4) A parallel passage of some importance is Colossians 1:28 where Paul speaks of his ministry and that of his colleagues like Epaphras who had brought the gospel to Colossae (1:7, 8). The Lord Jesus Christ who is at the centre of God's mystery, is the one who is proclaimed. Paul uses the weighty verb καταγγέλλω/ *katangellō* (in the present tense) to describe his ongoing proclamation of Christ as the centre of God's mystery; it has become almost a technical term for missionary preaching since it was normally used of the gospel or some element within it. This public proclamation of Christ as Lord is explained and developed in the following words about admonition and instruction, for it is through the *ongoing* teaching and warning of each person that the proclamation of Christ is carried out. Clearly for Paul and his colleagues evangelistic and missionary outreach was not achieved by some superficial presentation of the saving message about Christ to the world; rather, it was effected through warning and intensive teaching in pastoral situations. 'Proclaim' (καταγγέλλω/*katangellō*) in this context describes not simply the initial apostolic announcement, but draws attention to the ongoing and systematic presentation of Christ as Lord as well. This key verb which is used to cover of a broad range of activities, is employed similarly to εὐαγγελίζομαι/*euangelizomai*.

We conclude that when the apostle states he is 'eager to preach the gospel to you also in Rome' he has in mind the whole range of evangelistic and teaching ministry—from the initial proclamation of the gospel to the building up of believers and grounding them firmly in the faith. His language points to both primary evangelism and a full exposition of the gospel. The difficult expression, 'to you also', like the parallel 'among you' (v. 13), is employed rather loosely and is not limited exclusively to the readers. Accordingly, his apostolic labours will result in edification for the Roman Christians and conversions among others in the capital.

This comprehensive ambition now makes sense of Paul's unusual statement as to why he wants to visit Rome, namely, in order that he may *have some fruit* (καρπόν/*karpon*) *among them* as well as among the rest of the Gentiles (v. 13). The *fruit* is 'the return to be hoped for from apostolic labours, whether new converts gained or the strengthening of the faith and obedience of those already believing'.[31] And a rendering such as this is exactly in line with the goal of Paul's missionary calling, namely, to bring about 'the obedience of faith among all the Gentiles' (v. 5).[32]

(e) For I am not ashamed of the gospel (v. 16a).

Paul explains in the opening words of the letter's thematic statement (vv. 16-17, which shall be examined in detail later) why (γάρ/*gar*) he is so eager to preach the gospel in Rome: it is because he is not ashamed (ἐπαισχύνομαι/*epaischynomai*) of the gospel. These words have often been explained along psychological lines, indicating that Paul consciously thrust aside the natural feelings of shame which came upon him at the thought that he, an obscure provincial, was bearing a message that would inevitably be unacceptable in the Roman capital. While this may be true as far as it goes, it does not fully capture the meaning of the apostle's words.

The αἰσχύνομαι/*aischynomai* word-group (preceded by the negative 'not') turns up in a range of contexts within the Pauline letters where his apostleship and gospel—even his own life—are under threat.[33] In extremely adverse circumstances which he is not able to control, Paul states that he 'is/will not be ashamed' (cf. 2 Cor 10:8, where he is confronted with rivals in the church; Phil 1:20, where he awaits the outcome of his trial, which may lead to either life or death; cf. Rom 9:33; 10:1; 1 Cor 1:27; 2:3). Clearly, in each of these instances Paul's confidence does not, indeed cannot, reside in his circumstances; instead, it rests in God who has commissioned his servant as his accredited apostle and who works

31 C. E. B. Cranfield, *Romans* 1, 82. καρπός/*karpos* is applied in a variety of ways to the work of the apostle. The results of his missionary activity are his fruit (Phil 1:22); like a farmer he may partake of the fruit which has been produced through his ministry (2 Tim 2:6; 1 Cor 9:7), while the collection for the Jerusalem community is a fruit of the congregations in his mission (Rom 15:28). Elsewhere in the Pauline corpus καρπός/*karpos* signifies the 'result', 'outcome' or 'profit' of an action (Rom 6:21, 22; Gal 5:22; Eph 5:9; Phil 4:17), as it does in other writings of the New Testament. Cf. Mt. 21:43; Lk. 3:8; Jn. 15:5, 8, 16; Heb. 12:11; 13:15. See BAGD, 404-405.

32 Other suggestions as to what καρπός/*karpos* signifies include the 'fruit' of the Spirit (Gal 5:22), new converts, strengthening the Roman Christians, a contribution to Paul's collection for Jerusalem, assistance especially of some financial kind for his forthcoming visit to Spain, and some beneficial outcome of his visit to Rome which is not further specified.

33 See the important article of C. K. Barrett, 'I am not Ashamed of the Gospel', in *New Testament Essays* (London: SPCK, 1972), 116-143.

mightily through the gospel. Similarly, Paul's assertion in Romans 1:16a that he was not ashamed of the gospel explains why he was eager to preach it in Rome. He rejoiced in the gospel and his confidence lay in God who was powerfully at work in it, leading men and women to salvation.

To sum up. In the opening verse of Romans Paul speaks of his total involvement in the gospel. On the Damascus road God set him apart for the proclamation of the kerygma and from that moment on it became the dominant and determinative focus of his whole life. Perhaps in deliberate contrast to the cultic worship of the Jews this missionary states that he has given his life to the service of God in the preaching of the gospel of his Son (v. 9). The purpose of his missionary commission and of the apostolic gospel was the fulfilment of God's eternal plan of bringing Gentiles to 'the obedience of faith', that is, to bring about their glad submission to Jesus, the King of Israel. Paul's involvement in the gospel mission was the means by which, in the fulness of time, the risen Christ rules over the new people of God.

Because of his conviction that God was powerfully at work in the gospel, leading men and women to salvation, Paul was eager to preach this authoritative message in Rome. He was indebted to Greeks and to barbarians, to wise and to foolish, because of his obligation to Christ. Thus, his mission knew no limits. Furthermore, his total involvement in the gospel included the whole range of evangelistic and teaching activities—from its initial proclamation through to the grounding of believers firmly in the faith.

The Gospel in God's Saving Purposes

We have seen that Paul's involvement in the gospel was due to his calling and commission by God. Our study of Romans 1:1-17 (in addition to what has been observed in the first two chapters) has also suggested that his person and ministry were intimately linked with the apostolic kerygma because of its significant role in God's saving purposes. What, then, according to Romans 1, is the place and function of the gospel in salvation history? It is to this issue that we now turn.

(a) Promised beforehand in the OT Scriptures (vv. 1-2).

The gospel to which Paul has been set apart and is wholly committed is *God's* gospel—not in the sense that it is the message which speaks about him (an objective genitive), though this is true theologically. Rather, it is his gospel in that he is the source and authority of the message (θεοῦ/*theou*, 'of God', is a genitive of origin).[34] He is the one who has acted to bring salvation, to preserve his justice and to work out his purposes in history.[35]

Paul describes this divine proclamation further (by means of a relative clause 'which'), and makes three emphatic affirmations about it: (1) the gospel was promised beforehand, (2) through God's prophets, (3) in the OT scriptures. Clearly, the trustworthiness of the gospel is underlined by this expression—it is God who promised it. And because he had done this from of old the message is not a novel one. In this sense there is nothing new about the gospel, although it is appropriate to distinguish between the promise and its fulfilment.

By asserting that the gospel promises were 'through [God's] prophets in the holy scriptures', the apostle is not only stressing that the OT writings are the *place* where these promises are to be found. His affirmation *anchors the gospel in salvation history*. The OT scriptures contain the divine promises of the gospel; in addition, they reveal the unfolding purposes of God in significant events of that gospel which are announced, effected and divinely interpreted (e.g. the call of Abraham, the Exodus from Egypt and that from Babylon). God preserved in these holy writings both the announcements and the unfolding execution of his plan of salvation.[36]

The expression 'the holy scriptures' refers to the OT as a body of authoritative writings. At this point in Paul's opening no attempt is made to specify whether any particular scriptures of the OT are in view. Later in his thematic reference (1:16-17) and more detailed exposition (10:14-21; cf. 15:19-20) where he uses *gospel* terminology, the apostle focusses on material from Habakkuk (2:4) and Isaiah (52:7; 53:1; 65:1-2).

---

34   E. Molland, *Euangelion*, 156, J. A. Fitzmyer, 'The Gospel in the Theology of Paul', in *To Advance the Gospel* (New York: Crossroad, 1981), 151-152, L. Morris, *Romans*, 40, and J. D. G. Dunn, *Romans 1-8* , 10.

35   Note this emphasis in L. Morris' article, 'The Theme of Romans', in *Apostolic History and the Gospel. Biblical and Historical Essays Presented to F. F. Bruce*, ed. W. W. Gasque and R. P. Martin (Exeter: Paternoster, 1970), 249-263.

36   E. Käsemann, *Romans*, 9.

(b) The content of the gospel: Jesus Christ, Son of David and risen Son of God (vv. 3-4).

Paul now provides a succinct summary of the gospel's content: it is the message concerning God's Son, who is the Seed of David, Messiah and Lord. The Letter to the Romans contains no detailed christological discussion. Yet these verses with their important accumulation of titles are a reminder that the gospel cannot be understood apart from the person of Jesus Christ, who by his resurrection has inaugurated the new age of salvation.[37] This highly significant, though compressed, christological statement takes us to the heart of the gospel, which in turn will throw light on our inquiry into the place of the kerygma in the saving purposes of God.

This short confessional summary may have been a well-known formulation, or at least typical in its double affirmation ('Son of David', 'Son of God'), that struck a chord with the believers in Rome.[38] Even if it was as familiar to the Roman Christians as to Paul himself, it is possible he has 'recast its wording so as to bring out certain necessary emphases'.[39] At the same time its focus falls on the continuity between the OT and the gospel Paul preaches.

The title 'Son of God', which describes Jesus in a special way as an exalted, heavenly figure, turns up in Paul's letters only fifteen times. Yet it appears in important contexts in Galatians (1:15f.; 4:4f.), Romans (1:9; 8:3, 29, 32) and elsewhere (1 Cor 1:9; 15:58; 2 Cor 1:18; 1 Thess 1:10), where it consistently highlights Jesus' saving significance. Hengel concludes his careful examination that in almost all his statements about the Son of God, 'Paul uses the title *when he is speaking of the close bond between Jesus Christ and God, that is, of his function as the mediator of salvation* between God and man'.[40]

Although this confession in Romans 1:3-4 does not in itself imply the pre-existence or the sending of the Son of God, this was an essential element in Paul's Son Christology (cf. Rom 8:3; Gal

---

37 D. Moo, *Romans 1-8*, 43.

38 The arguments for vv. 3b-4 being a primitive Christian creed turn on the structure of the section, the reference to David, some un-Pauline vocabulary and supposed theological implications which some find difficult to ascribe to Paul (e.g. a pre-Pauline adoptionist Christology). But the credal hypothesis is open to criticism and is not as certain as has been suggested.

39 F. F. Bruce, *Romans*, 72.

40 M. Hengel, *The Son of God* (London: SCM, 1976), 10 (his emphasis).

4:4; Col 1:13ff.)[41] and it is confirmed by the closure of his confession with the appositional words, 'Jesus Christ our Lord'.

By means of two lines in antithetic parallelism, in which the 'flesh-spirit'[42] contrast of Paul's salvation historical framework appears, the apostle makes two affirmations about the Son of God:[43]

(1) In Jesus' earthly life he was the seed of David, the Messiah (v. 3). He fulfils the prophetic hopes of the people of Israel for the age to come (the promise to David that his seed would have an eternal reign, 2 Sam 7:12-16, became a particular focus of messianic expectation in the OT: cf. Isa 11; Jer 23:5-6; 33:14-18; Ezek 34:23-31; 37:24-28). As such he goes to his death.[44]

(2) By virtue of his resurrection Jesus is appointed as Son of God in power (v. 4). With this mighty event the inauguration of the new age has begun. His resurrection fulfils the words of Psalm 2:7, which speak of the coronation of the Davidic King, and in this new stage of God's plan Jesus rules as the powerful, life-giving Son of God. He has become the ruling heir of the nations of Psalm 2:8,[45] and is mightily active to bring salvation to all who believe (cf. 1:16).[46]

Thus, he who is the unique Son of God, the mediator of salvation between God and man, was in his earthly life the Seed of David, the Messiah. By his resurrection he has become the powerful Son of God—Jesus Christ, our Lord.

(c) The purpose of the gospel: the risen Christ's rule over the new people of God (v. 5).

We have already seen that the purpose of Paul's missionary commission, as well as that of his apostolic gospel, was 'to bring

---

41 Against J. D. G. Dunn who has consistently argued against the notion of preexistence in Paul's christology; cf. his *Christology in the Making* (London: SCM, 1980), 98-128.

42 Greek: σάρξ-πνεῦμα/*sarx-pneuma*.

43 Cf. M. Hengel, *Son of God*, 59-66, and S. Kim, *Origin*, 111-114.

44 M. Hengel, *Son of God*, 61, 'The death of Jesus is only presupposed implicitly in the statement about the resurrection'.

45 D. B. Garlington, '*The Obedience of Faith*', 236.

46 L. W. Hurtado, *One God, One Lord* (Philadelphia: Fortress, 1988), 93-99, interprets Rom 1:1-4, along with a number of other passages (1 Thess 1:9-10; 1 Cor 15:20-28; Phil 2:5-11; 1 Cor 8:1-6), as evidence of 'the earliest christological conviction . . . that the risen Jesus had been made God's chief agent' (95). This is an important ingredient in Hurtado's explanation as to how Jesus became the object of early Christian devotion within the context of ancient Jewish monotheism.

about the obedience of faith among all the Gentiles for the sake of the name of Christ' (1:5). We noted that this programmatic statement draws attention to the purpose, sphere and person on whose behalf the totality of Paul's missionary endeavours were being pursued. 'God is *now* bringing his purposes to pass in salvation history through Paul's gospel, i.e. the preaching of Jesus Christ [16:25]'.[47] As the apostle proclaims this authoritative message, 'Jesus, the king of Israel, takes the nations in captive obedience to himself (Gen 49:10; Ps 2:8f.)'. The gospel thus preached is the means 'by which the risen Christ in the fullness of time asserts his rule over the new people of God'.[48]

(d) The saving power of the gospel—God's promises to Abraham are fulfilled (vv. 16-17).

With verses 16 and 17 we come to the thematic statement of the entire letter: the saving power of the gospel to everyone who believes. Paul shifts the focus from his own ministry (v. 16a), the very essence of which has been the gospel (vv. 1, 9, 15), to what the gospel achieves (vv. 16b–17). In this highly significant passage two important and closely related motifs call for attention as we seek to determine the place of this dynamic message in God's purposes: first, the saving power of the gospel and, secondly, the fulfilment of God's covenant promises to Abraham in the gospel. The following brief exposition will concentrate on these closely associated themes.

(1) These key verses are the climax of Paul's introduction (1:1–17) and provide the theme for what follows in the letter. They therefore function as an important hinge. Leon Morris aptly remarks: 'These two verses have an importance out of all proportion to their length. The weighty matter they contain tells us much of what this epistle is about'.[49]

---

47   D. B. Garlington, 'The Obedience of Faith', 205 (his emphasis).
48   D. B. Garlington, 'The Obedience of Faith', 203.
49   L. Morris, *Romans*, 66. Cf. J. D. G. Dunn, *Romans 1-8*, 37, and D. Moo, *Romans 1-8*, 59–60. Against E. R. and P. Achtemaier, 'Righteousness', *IDB* 4, 80–85, 91–99, who claim that vv. 16–17 and 18ff. are grammatically subordinate to v. 15, so that Paul's words about his eagerness to preach the gospel in Rome are thought to be the main statement, with vv. 16–17 supportive of this. This is to overload the significance of the γάρ/*gar* ('for'), which does not specifically indicate where the emphasis lies. A subordinate clause in Greek often stands out in importance because of its content and there is no reason to depart from the usual interpretation which sees vv. 16–17 as the climax of the introduction and theme for what follows.

(2) The ground or reason (γάρ/*gar*) for Paul's not being ashamed to confess the gospel is that this apparently weak and foolish message, the content of which centres on Jesus Christ, mediates the almighty power of God that leads to salvation. It is not that the gospel simply speaks about divine power; *it is God's power* leading to deliverance on the last day. This notion of the message being an effective power (cf. 1 Cor 1:18) is to be understood in the light of such OT passages concerning the divine word as Genesis 1:3, 6, etc.; Psalm 147:15; Isaiah 40:8b; 55:10-11; and Jeremiah 23:29.

In Paul's letters the 'salvation' word-group (σώζω/*sōzō*, and σωτηρία/*sōteria*) is used only in connection with mankind's relations with God. The terms have primarily an eschatological reference (1 Cor 5:5; cf. Rom 5:9-10; 13:11; 1 Cor 3:15; Phil 1:28; 2:12; 1 Thess 5:8-9; 2 Thess 2:13). Negatively, they speak of a deliverance from God's wrath in the final judgment (Rom 5:9) and, positively, of the reinstatement in that glory of God which was lost through sin (Rom 8:30). While salvation is usually spoken of in future tenses, Paul can refer to it as past (Eph 2:5, 8; cf. Rom 8:24), since the decisive act of God by which the believer's final salvation is secured has already been accomplished.

(3) The seriousness of humanity's predicament outside of Christ and apart from his gospel is made devastatingly clear in the following context of vv. 18-32, where Paul speaks of a world under judgment. The wrath of God is revealed from heaven against all ungodliness and wickedness of those who by their wickedness suppress the truth (v. 18).

NT scholarship is divided as to whether the revelation of God's wrath (1:18) and the universal indictment of humanity which follows in 1:18–3:20 are part of the gospel itself or an interruption to Paul's exposition of that gospel. (a) In favour of the former, K. Barth and C. E. B. Cranfield have argued that the revelation of God's holy anger is not that which occurs in the frustrations, futilities and disasters as a result of human godlessness and wickedness. Rather, the parallelism between vv. 17 and 18 indicates that the most natural way of taking the latter is to understand Paul to mean that the wrath of God is also being revealed in the gospel, that is, in the on-going proclamation of the gospel, and to recognize that behind, and basic to, this revelation of the wrath of God in the preaching is the prior revelation of the wrath of God in the gospel events. The two revelations are two aspects of the same process.[50] (b) However, in spite of the cogency with which this interpretation is presented, it is open to a number of criticisms.[51] So we conclude that when he speaks of the wrath of God being revealed Paul is describing a process that is going on before his eyes in the events of human experience.

But whether we follow the traditional view that Paul is describing an ongoing process in which the wrath of God is revealed in the events of human experience, or a revelation of holy anger that occurs in the preaching of the gospel, it is clear that mankind outside of Christ and his gospel lies under divine judgment. In contrast, then, the mighty salvation of God by which men and women are delivered from this judgment stands out all the more clearly as being truly glorious.

(4) If we ask the question as to how the gospel is God's saving power to everyone who believes, then v. 17 with its introductory 'for' (γάρ/*gar*) gives the answer. The gospel is God's saving power to everyone who believes *because* in it there is a revelation of the righteousness of God (δικαιοσύνη θεοῦ/*dikaiosunē theou*). Paul is stating that 'the gospel in some way actually makes manifest, or brings into existence, "the righteousness of God"'.[52] This takes place in the ongoing preaching of the gospel, as the present tense, 'is being revealed' (ἀποκαλύπτεται/*apokalyptetai*), suggests.[53] The

---

50   See the exposition of C. E. B. Cranfield, *Romans* 1, 110, who points out that on this interpretation (1) the parallelism of the two verses is most satisfactorily preserved, (2) γάρ/*gar* has its normal meaning of 'for', and (3) 'from heaven' which underlines the expression 'of God', emphasizes the utter seriousness of this wrath and makes plain that it is indeed God's wrath.

51   First, while at one level the Barth-Cranfield view appears to do justice to the parallelism of vv. 17 and 18, it requires ἀποκαλύπτεται/*apokalyptetai* at v. 18 to be understood in a cognitive sense ('make known, disclose'), but the same verb in v. 17 has the meaning 'manifest [an action] in history', so breaking the parallelism. Consequently, it is better to understand the verb in v. 18 as 'manifest [an action] in history', since the object of this revealing is not people but their sins. Secondly, while the apostle does not usually include in the gospel the negative ideas of judgment and wrath (though cf. 2:16), if in the light of v. 16 he had done so, one might have expected some kind of indication in the context, such as 'in it also [i.e. in the gospel]'. Note the arguments of D. Moo, *Romans 1-8*, 95.

52   D. Moo, *Romans 1-8*, 65. The verb 'reveal' (ἀποκαλύπτω/*apokalyptō*) here denotes the 'uncovering' of God's saving plan, as it unfolds in human history (cf. Rom 2:5; 8:18, 19; 1 Cor 1:7; Gal 1:16; 3:23; 2 Thess 1:7; 2:3, 6, 8).

53   The difference with Romans 3:21 is that the perfect tense, '[the righteousness of God] has been made manifest' (πεφανέρωται/*pephanerōtai*), focusses on the cross 'as the time of God's decisive intervention to establish his righteousness', D. Moo, *Romans 1-8*, 65.

passive voice points to the fact that God is the one at work: it is he who brings into existence his righteousness. He is causing his righteousness to be experienced, by Gentiles and Jews who believe. And that continuing revelation of God's righteousness 'through the proclamation of the Law-free gospel is bound up with the consummation of his purpose in history'.[54]

In spite of lively, diverse and even heated theological debate, no scholarly consensus has been reached as to the meaning of 'the righteousness of God' in Paul—either generally or specifically in this passage. δικαιοσύνη θεοῦ/*dikaiosynē theou* has been taken to refer to (1) *a status given by God* (with θεοῦ/*theou* as a genitive of source ['righteousness *from* God'], or an objective genitive ['righteousness that is valid before God']), (2) *an activity of God* (θεοῦ/*theou* is a subjective genitive), or (3) *God's justice* or *his faithfulness*—to his covenant with Israel, or to his creation as a whole (θεοῦ/*theou* is a possessive genitive). A particularly powerful interpretation has been E. Käsemann's combination: he argues that 'God's righteousness' is his 'salvation-creating power', which incorporates the notions of status given by God and especially the activity exercised by him.

We have examined the complex issues and arguments surrounding this debate elsewhere.[55] On the whole our preference is for the line adopted by S. K. Williams who claims that 'the righteousness of God' (as distinct from 'righteousness')[56] is an expression which brings to mind that aspect of God's nature which describes his steadfast adherence to what is right and fitting, his constancy and trustworthiness. From a careful study of several key texts in Romans (chaps. 3, 4, apart from 1:16-17)[57] and Galatians

---

54 S. K. Williams, 'The "Righteousness of God" in Romans', *JBL* 99 (1980), 256. Cf. J. D. G. Dunn, *Romans 1-8*, 48: 'Paul's experience of evangelizing the Gentiles gives him firm confidence that in the gospel as the power of God to salvation such early converts are being given to see the righteousness of God actually happening, taking effect in their own conversion'.

55 'Justification in Paul and Some Crucial Issues of the Last Two Decades', in *Right with God: Justification in the Bible and the World*, ed. D.A. Carson (Carlisle: Paternoster, 1992), 69-95, 263-268.

56 Which can be used to describe a gift from God (i.e. a righteous status). Paul speaks about the free gift of righteousness (Rom 5:17), or of righteousness having been received or attained (cf. Rom 4; 5:21; 8:10; 9:30; 10:4, 10; 14:17).

57 To take one example, S. K. Williams ('The "Righteousness of God"', 267) argues that 'the oracles of God' (Rom 3:2) refers first and foremost to the promises given to Abraham (chap. 4) and confirmed by the prophets (cf. 1:16-17; 9:25-26, 33; 10:11, 20).

(chap. 3), Williams fills out the content of the phrase and claims that it denotes God's faithfulness to his covenant promises to Abraham (θεοῦ/*theou* is thus a subjective genitive). Those promises to Abraham were that through his descendants he would be 'the heir of the world' (cf. Gen 22:17; 12:7; 13:15; 15:18; 26:3). Gentiles were now coming to be included within the people of God through Paul's (and others') preaching of the gospel, and this new people was extending across the world. Abraham's spiritual descendants would become as numerous as the stars of heaven (cf. Rom 4:18 with Gen 15:15) and so would become the heirs of the world. By justifying all people of the earth through faith God keeps his promise to Abraham and demonstrates his righteousness in the eschatological present time (Rom 3:26).[58]

According to Williams, Paul's use here of Habakkuk 2:4 is nothing less than 'the prophetic summary of the gospel'. He cites the quotation as scriptural proof for several of the key ideas in vv. 16-17.[59] At Romans 1:2 the apostle had stated that God 'promised the gospel beforehand through his prophets in the holy scriptures'. He now quotes in v. 17 some of those all-important words from one of the prophets that are preserved in scripture, and affirms that 'he who is righteous by faith shall live [that is, in God's presence, at the end]'. Understood in this way the text is consistent with this interpretation of 'the righteousness of God'.

To conclude. Our examination of the place of the gospel in the saving purposes of God has been necessarily brief. We have limited our inquiry to the introduction of Romans (1:1-17) rather than the whole letter. Nevertheless, the results of this short investigation are important. In saying that the gospel of God was promised beforehand in the OT scriptures (v. 2), the apostle is asserting that these authoritative writings reveal the unfolding purposes of God in significant events of the gospel; these events are announced, effected and divinely interpreted in the scriptures. In particular, Habakkuk 2:4 is cited as scriptural proof for key ideas in Romans 1:16-17 and is a prophetic summary of the gospel, affirming that 'he who through faith is righteous shall live [that is, in God's presence, at the end]'.

---

58   S. K. Williams, 'The "Righteousness of God"', 279-280.

59   'By faith[fulness]' in Hab 2:4 echoes the same expression in Rom 1:17a, as well as the 'everyone who believes' of v. 16, while the 'shall live' with its eschatological reference alludes to 'to salvation' of v. 16.

The saving power of the gospel needs to be understood in the light of humanity's dreadful predicament outside of Christ. The world stands under judgment, 'for the wrath of God is revealed from heaven against all ungodliness and wickedness' of men and women (Rom 1:18). Salvation is deliverance from divine wrath on the final day and reinstatement in the glory of God which was lost through sin. The gospel is God's saving power for everyone who believes because in it there is a revelation of the righteousness of God. In the proclamation of this authoritative message God acquits the guilty, whether they are Jew or Gentile, on the basis of Christ's death (Rom 3:21-26). Salvation thus becomes effective for everyone who believes, both Jew and Gentile. God's covenant promises to Abraham are revealed in this authoritative announcement and find their fulfilment. Gentiles along with Jews become children of Abraham.

Central to the place of the gospel in the saving purposes of God is the person and work of Jesus Christ. He is at the heart of God's redemptive plan. These purposes find their fulfilment, climax and consummation in the saving work of God's Messiah. Jesus Christ is the unique Son of God who is the mediator of salvation between God and man. In his earthly life he was the Seed of David, the Messiah, who fulfils the prophetic hopes of the people of Israel for the age to come. By his resurrection he was installed as Son of God in power. With this mighty event the new age has begun. His resurrection fulfils the words of Psalm 2:7, and in this new stage of God's plan he rules as the powerful, life-giving Son of God. Jesus as the King of Israel takes the nations into captive obedience to himself and in the fulness of time rules over them as the new people of God.

Constrained by the Gospel

We have studied Romans 1:1-17 in order to examine the claim that the 'gospel' provides the connecting link between Paul's activity and that of other Christians. This was part of a wider inquiry into Paul's theology of mission. We looked first at his own involvement in the gospel and, then, at the place of this authoritative message within God's saving purposes.

The theme of Paul's total involvement in the gospel runs like a scarlet thread throughout the letter, from the first verse to the concluding doxology. From the time of his conversion and calling on the Damascus road, when God set him apart for the gospel, it became the dominant and determinative focus of his whole life. Paul also knew that God was powerfully at work in the gospel, leading men and women to salvation. This authoritative message, as we have seen in so many different ways, was inextricably linked with God's redemptive purposes. Indeed, one could almost identify that gospel with the saving purposes of God. Paul was thus wholly committed to the kerygma, *not simply* because of his own conversion and calling by God to minister to Gentiles, *but also* because of the essential place of the gospel in salvation history.

Paul's missionary activity, as we have seen, was part of a larger whole. His own involvement in the gospel led to the ingathering of Gentiles into the covenant people of God. But the ingathering of the nations was vaster and greater than Paul's own contribution, however vital this was. Likewise the advance of the gospel in which he was significantly involved was occurring throughout the world, in the places where Paul was actively engaged *and* where others were hard at work evangelizing. We therefore believe that the gospel does serve as the bridge between Paul's and other Christians' activities and that it is the key to understanding the relationship between the apostle's teaching about his mission and that of mission generally.

The Letter to the Romans was written apparently for a number of related purposes. NT scholarship has not yet reached a consensus as to precisely what those purposes were. One can affirm, however, that the apostle's exposition of the gospel in this letter and its essential place within redemptive history was intended to instruct the Roman Christians. Paul wanted these believers in the capital to understand (more fully) the saving power of the gospel against the backdrop of a world that was lost and under judgment. He instructed them so that they might know more clearly about the Son of God as the mediator of salvation who in his role as the King of Israel brings Gentiles into captive obedience to himself. And Paul desired that they might comprehend God's faithfulness to his covenant promises to Abraham in bringing Gentiles along with Jews into his family.

A number of important implications flow from these conclusions:

(1) The dynamic of the gospel's logic meant for these believers in Rome and for other Christians, including ourselves, a deeper commitment to its ongoing, powerful advance, as well as to the

person at its centre, Jesus Christ, God's Son. If we have understood that Jesus Christ is at the heart of God's redemptive plan and that the divine purposes find their fulfilment, climax and consummation in his saving work, then we who have come under his rule as Lord must be wholly committed to the furtherance of those saving purposes in which Gentiles, along with Jews, are brought into obedience to him.

(2) We who have truly experienced the saving power of the gospel in our own lives and have the assurance of deliverance from the wrath to come on the final day, cannot be anything other than debtors to those for whom Christ died—just as Paul was a debtor to them. If we know the desperate plight of men and women under divine judgment—we ourselves had once been in this predicament—and that the gospel is the only hope for deliverance from the wrath to come, then we should be wholly involved in bringing it into the lives of others.

(3) This is not to suggest that other Christians have the same calling to ministry as Paul, that their gifts of evangelism are identical with his, or that they are to be itinerant and roving missionaries like the apostle to the Gentiles. But men and women over whom Christ rules as Lord are to be wholly committed to him and his gospel with its dynamic onward march. This is the logic of Paul's gospel; if he was constrained by this divinely powerful message, then so should we be.

Appendix C. The Background to Paul's Use of
εὐαγγέλιον/*euangelion*[60]

(a) Introduction

The εὐαγγελ/*euangel* word-group turns up in the Pauline corpus on some eighty-four occasions: the noun εὐαγγέλιον/

---

60 Note especially P. Stuhlmacher, *Das paulinische Evangelium. I. Vorgeschichte* (Göttingen: Vandenhoeck, 1968), and 'The Theme: The Gospel and the Gospels', in *The Gospel and the Gospels,* ed. P. Stuhlmacher (Grand Rapids: Eerdmans, 1991), 1-25, 'The Pauline Gospel', in *Gospel and the Gospels,* 149-172; H. Schlier, 'Εὐαγγέλιον im Römerbrief', in *Wort Gottes in der Zeit,* ed. K. Feld and J. Nolte (Dusseldorf: Patmos, 1973), 127-142; U. Wilckens, *Der Brief an die Römer. Röm 1-5* (Zürich/Einsiedeln/Köln: Benziger, 1978; Neukirchen: Neukirchener Verlag, 1978), 74-75; P. T. O'Brien, 'The Importance of the Gospel in Philippians', in *God who is Rich in Mercy. Essays presented to D. B. Knox,* ed. P. T. O'Brien and D. G. Peterson (Homebush West, NSW: Lancer, 1986), 213-233; and H. Merklein, 'Zum Verständnis des paulinischen Begriffs "Evangelium"', in *Studien zu Jesus und Paulus* (Tübingen: Mohr, 1987), 279-295.

euangelion ('gospel') is used some sixty times, the verb εὐαγγελίζομαι/*euangelizomai* ('preach the gospel') twenty-one times, with the noun εὐαγγελιστής/*euangelistēs* ('evangelist') twice (Eph 4:11; 2 Tim 4:5) and the related verb προευαγγελίζομαι/ *proeuangelizomai* ('preach the gospel beforehand') once (at Gal 3:8). Surprisingly, these terms appear less frequently in the rest of the NT. For example, εὐαγγέλιον/*euangelion* turns up on only sixteen other occasions, half of which are in Mark, while the verb εὐαγγελίζομαι/*euangelizomai* (apart from the instances in Luke: Gospel 10, Acts 15) occurs only eight additional times.

In general, εὐαγγέλιον/*euangelion* served as a label to express in summary fashion the message that Paul announced to the world of his day (Rom 1:1).[61] Although the term and its cognates occupied a significant place in Pauline teaching, he was not the first to employ this language. Prior to his ministry εὐαγγελίζομαι/ *euangelizomai* was already a technical term in early Christian vocabulary to denote the authoritative news of Jesus Christ.

(b) The Graeco-Roman world

εὐαγγέλιον/*euangelion* originally signified 'the reward' given to a messenger for his tidings, especially his good news which brought relief to his recipients. The term then came to be used of the message itself. While occasionally signifying political and private messages, it had importance as a message of victory and this was often understood as a gift of the gods. On such occasions sacrifices were offered to the gods out of gratitude and in order to secure the benefits proclaimed by the 'good news'.

Of special importance are those instances of the plural εὐαγγέλια/*euangelia* in the language of the imperial cult to describe the emperor's birth, coming of age or enthronement as well as his speeches, decrees and acts that were regarded as the 'glad tidings' which brought the long hoped-for fulfilment to the longings of the world for happiness and peace. The oft-quoted Calendar Inscription from Priene (in Asia Minor) says 'the birthday of the god [= Augustus] was for the world the beginning of *good tidings* owing to him'. The proclamation of these tidings does not

---

61   'Gospel' became 'a central concept of Paul's theology; it was for the apostle the principal, theologically-charged motif in his mission preaching', U. Wilckens, *Röm 1-5*, 74, and H. Merklein, 'Zum Verständnis', 279.

simply herald the new era; it actually brings it about. While earlier scholarship was inclined to interpret the early Christians' use of the singular εὐαγγελίζομαι/*euangelizomai* against this background of the imperial cult, this assessment is currently regarded as unlikely: in the latter context only the plural (εὐαγγέλια/*euangelia*) appears, not a technical singular, while the NT itself gives no evidence of a political or polemical orientation.

(c) The OT background

Of greater significance than the imperial cult for an understanding of the background to Paul's thought is the cognate verb εὐαγγελίζομαι/*euangelizomai* (particularly in Isaiah 40-66) which comes to stand for the Hebrew *biśśēr*, 'to announce, tell, deliver a (good or bad) message' (e.g. 1 Kings 1:42; Jer 20:15). This verb is used in the Psalms. 40:9[10]; 68:11[12]; 96:2ff. and Isaiah 41:27; 52:7 to herald Yahweh's victory over the world and his kingly rule. With his enthronement (cf. esp. Ps 96) and his return to Zion (Isa 40ff.) a new era begins. The messenger of good tidings, the *m^e baśśēr* (rendered by ὁ εὐαγγελιζόμενος/*ho euangelizomenos* in the LXX), announces this new era of God's rule and inaugurates it by his word. The Lord has become king (Isa 52:7; cf. 40:9; 41:27) and his reign extends over the whole earth (Ps 96:2ff.). Peace and salvation have now come. In the mouth of his messengers God himself speaks and through this divine proclamation the new age begins.

(d) Jesus and his disciples

Jesus understood his own sending in the light of Isaiah 61:1-2, for according to Matthew 11:2-6 he regarded his healing miracles and his preaching as a fulfilment of this OT text (cf. Isa 35).[62] He saw himself as the messianic evangelist of the poor (Matt. 11:5), fulfilling the role of the *m^e baśśēr* ('messenger of good tidings') of whom Isaiah 61:1 speaks. His preaching of God's kingly rule (Mark 1:15) is the *b^e śōrâh* = 'message of peace' of Isaiah 52:7 ('How beautiful upon the mountains are the feet of the messenger who announces peace, who brings good news, who announces salvation,

---

62   See the careful treatment of this by P. Stuhlmacher, 'The Theme: The Gospel and the Gospels', 20-21.

who says to Zion, "Your God reigns'"). His gospel announcement is the *ś^emû'âh* ('report') of Isaiah 53:1, that is, the saving message of God's coming. The term εὐαγγέλιον/*euangelion* is attributed to Jesus by the evangelists on a number of occasions (Mark 1:15; 8:35; 10:29; 13:10; 14:9; Matt 4:23; 9:35; 24:14; 26:13). Further, Jesus 'appears not only as the messenger and the author of the message, but at the same time as its subject, the one of whom the message tells'.[63] It is therefore not surprising that the NT writers apply the term εὐαγγέλιον/*euangelion* to describe the message of salvation that is connected with the coming of Jesus. He is the messenger who announces the arrival of peace and salvation with the coming of God himself.

Jesus' disciples shared in his proclamation and saw their task as a continuation of that of the *m^ebaśśēr* ('messenger') of Isaiah 61:1ff. and 52:7 (cf. Matt 10:1-16; Luke 9:6).

(e) Early Christian preaching

Both the singular noun 'gospel' and the cognate verb were employed to describe the early Christian preaching of the coming of God's rule as evidenced in the coming of Jesus, his death and resurrection (cf. Acts 5:32), a gospel that was for both Jew and Gentile alike. The mission preaching of Peter is referred to by means of εὐαγγέλιον/*euangelion* (Acts 15:7; cf. that of Paul: Acts 20:24), while in chap. 10:36ff., where the account of Peter's preaching the gospel to Cornelius is reported, the verb 'preach the gospel' is used in a significant way. Echoes of Isaiah 52:7 (cf. Nah 2:1) can be heard, while God himself is named as the messenger (εὐαγγελιζόμενος/*euangelizomenos*) of peace through Jesus Christ (v 36).

(f) Summary conclusion

Prior to Paul's ministry εὐαγγέλιον/*euangelion* was already a technical term in early Christian vocabulary to denote the authoritative news of Jesus Christ. The apostle's frequent use of the noun 'gospel' absolutely (that is, without any qualifiers) indicates that he was taking over phraseology already familiar to his readers. They knew what the content of the gospel was (cf. 1 Cor 15:1ff.).

---

63   U. Becker, *NIDNTT* 2, 110.

The noun could describe the activity of preaching the gospel as well as the content of the message.

The Christian use of the word derives from Jesus' own ministry in which the verb form was established in dependence on Isaiah 61:1, 2 (cf. 40:9; 52:7). Jesus understood his own ministry as a fulfilment of the role of the *m^ebaśśēr* of Isaiah. He is the messenger who announces the arrival of peace and salvation with the coming of God himself. Further, Jesus' disciples shared in his proclamation and saw their task as a continuation of that of the *m^ebaśśēr* of Isaiah 61:1ff. and 52:7.

CHAPTER 4

PAUL'S AMBITIONS AND OURS

1 Corinthians 9:19-23; 10:31-11:1

Introduction: Paul as a Model

The apostle Paul presents himself on a number of occasions in his letters as a model to be followed by his readers. Four times in his Epistle to the Philippians he calls upon his Christian friends to emulate his own example: he wants them to have the same attitude of mind in relation to their ultimate goals (Phil 3:15), to be united in imitating him and to pay careful attention to others following the apostolic pattern (3:17). Finally, he urges them to put into practice the things which they had learnt and received from him (4:9; cf. 2:17).[1] As he writes to his Christian friends at Thessalonica he positively claims: 'You became imitators of us and of the Lord' (1 Thess 1:6). By imitating him the Thessalonians had joined Paul in suffering affliction (cf. 2:14), as well as in love and in the giving of themselves to others.

Additional examples in the apostle's letters could be cited to illustrate the point that Paul presents himself as a model to be followed, not only by his fellow-workers, but also by all in his churches (cf. 1 Cor 4:16; 10:31–11:1; Eph 5:1; 1 Thess 2:14; 2 Thess 3:7-9). A. J. Malherbe comments: 'Paul's method of shaping a community was to gather converts around himself and by his own

---

1   See P. T. O'Brien, 'The Gospel and Godly Models in Philippians', in *Worship, Theology and Ministry in the Early Church. Essays in Honor of Professor Ralph P. Martin*, ed. M. J. Wilkins and T. Paige (Sheffield: Academic Press, 1992), 273–284. For bibliographical details see my commentary *The Epistle to the Philippians* (Grand Rapids: Eerdmans, 1991), 442-443, in addition to the recent article of E. A. Judge, 'The Teacher as Moral Exemplar in Paul and in the Inscriptions of Ephesus', *In the Fullness of Time: Biblical Studies in Honour of Archbishop Donald Robinson*, ed. D. G. Peterson and J. Pryor (Homebush West, NSW: Lancer, 1992), 185-201.

behavior to demonstrate what he taught'.[2] According to Malherbe he was following a method widely practised by the moral philosophers, in particular. The teacher as model provided a moral paradigm. In addition to this, according to Seneca, he offered security to those who turned to him for guidance (Seneca *Epistle* 11.8-10).[3]

Consistent with Christian Humility?

The question immediately arises as to whether Paul's choice of himself as a model for godly behaviour is truly consistent with Christian humility. The following points are pertinent:

(1) The apostle tells his readers at Philippi that Christ Jesus is the example par excellence (Phil 2:5-11) and that their attitude and behaviour should be like his. Paul himself is a model in so far as he follows the 'Lordly Example' of Jesus himself. This is consistent with his statement to the Corinthians that he was extremely careful about his conduct. He did not wish to become, either wittingly or unwittingly, a stumbling block to others and lead them into sin. He urged his Corinthian converts to be equally careful: 'Do not cause anyone to stumble, whether Jews, Greeks or the church of God—even as I try to please everybody in every way. For I am not seeking my own good but the good of many, so that they may be saved. Follow my example, as I follow the example of Christ' (1 Cor 10:32–11:1).

(2) Paul was not placing himself on a pedestal, as though he was 'perfect' or had already arrived at the eschaton (contrast some at Corinth, 1 Cor 4:7, 8). On the contrary, he disclaimed having reached perfection (Phil 3:12-14) whatever others, who were having an adverse influence on the congregation at Philippi, might claim for themselves. He keeps on pursuing his long-cherished ambition of perfectly laying hold of Christ and he wants the Philippians to do the same. He is thus an example in his orientation and attitude (cf. 3:15) as well as his behaviour (v. 16).

2　A. J. Malherbe, *Paul and the Thessalonians* (Philadelphia: Fortress, 1987), 52. Note also the discussion of O. Haas, *Paulus*, 69-79, in the context of Paul as a missionary model.

3　E. A. Judge, 'The Teacher as Moral Exemplar', 191-197, has argued, however, that 'Paul's call for imitation is unique' (191) because it arises from the context of preaching the gospel and has to do with an imitation in affliction.

(3) The apostle includes others along with himself as the kind of example the Philippians are to imitate. He has already held up Timothy (Phil 2:19-24) and Epaphroditus (2:25-30) as godly models to follow—living examples of those who 'have the mind' of Christ Jesus. At chap. 3:17 he changes from the singular to the plural ('us') to include others along with himself: 'Be united in imitating me and pay careful attention to *those* who live according to the pattern *we* gave you'. Paul's was no arrogant claim which demanded that his readers should follow in his magnificent steps! In this context W. P. De Boer's remarks are worth quoting at length:

> The Christian walk was not merely one man's peculiarities, but the consistent pattern of Paul and his associates, seen both when they were all together, and when only various of the associates revisited Philippi. Hence, this Christian pattern had been held before them more than once. It had been stamped on their minds repeatedly and under various circumstances by Paul and his associates. There were presently leaders in Philippi who were themselves conforming to this Christian pattern. Paul directs his readers' attention to them . . . [he] is intent on appealing to the Christian pattern on as broad a base as possible.[4]

(4) It is clear from the following verses (Phil 3:18–19) that there were, in fact, other models who were setting a bad example and having the wrong kind of influence on the Philippian church. Theirs was the absolute antithesis of the Pauline model. They showed by their behaviour (περιπατοῦσιν/*peripatousin*, 'walk') that they deliberately repudiated all that the cross of Christ stood for (v. 18). Paul is obviously anxious that godly examples be clearly presented to the readers so that they will have a powerful influence on both their attitudes and behaviour.

In the light of these factors, then, we conclude that Paul's choice of himself as a pattern to be followed was consistent with Christian humility.

---

4   W. P. De Boer, *The Imitation of Paul* (Kampen: Kok, 1962), 183.

A Model for What Purposes?

It was natural that the apostle's converts should look to him for guidance. After all, he was the minister (διάκονος / *diakonos*) through whom they had believed (cf. 1 Cor 3:5), thus enabling them to come into a new relationship with the living God (cf. 1 Thess 1:8-9). But what functions do these references in his letters to himself as a model serve? What points is he making by using himself as an example?

Most are agreed that when Paul reminds his readers of his pattern of behaviour he does so for practical and exhortatory purposes since he has an ethical dimension in view.[5] We know, for example, that when he preached the gospel he usually provided for his own material needs by carrying on his own trade as a tentmaker or leatherworker. He did this so as not to be a burden on his converts (1 Cor 4:12; 9:6; 1 Thess 2:9; 2 Thess 3:8).[6] But does Paul have simply an ethical vista in view when he speaks of himself as an example? Is there something additional, perhaps even related to the gospel of the Lord Jesus which is so dominant in Paul's life?

In an attempt to take some initial soundings we turn to Paul's words on this theme of his being a model to two churches he had founded, namely, at Philippi and Thessalonica:

(a) Paul as a Model to the Philippians

We have argued elsewhere that in the Letter to the Philippians Paul's references to himself as an example serve several different, though closely related, functions which tie in with his *central exhortation* in the letter, 'Now, the important thing is this: live as citizens of heaven in a manner that is worthy of the gospel of Christ' (Phil 1:27). This itself is part of the leading proposition to persevere and stand firm (1:27-30).[7] Paul's being a model is linked with the gospel of the Lord Jesus, particularly with a manner of life that is consistent with that kerygma.

---

5   Note, however, the recent caveats of E. A. Judge, 'The Teacher as Moral Exemplar', 191-197.

6   O. Haas, *Paulus*, 70-72.

7   P. T. O'Brien, 'The Gospel and Godly Models', 273–284; see also the relevant exegetical comments on 2:17; 3:15, 17; 4:9 in my commentary, *The Epistle to the Philippians* (Grand Rapids: Eerdmans, 1991).

The reference to Paul's willingness to be 'poured out as a libation' over the Philippians' sacrifice (2:17) seems to play only a subordinate role as a model. He has already presented the example of Christ's lowly service (2:5-11) as a powerful corrective to the readers' undue concern about their own interests (v. 4). He now mentions his own example before passing on to the powerful models of Timothy (2:20-22) and Epaphroditus (2:30). As a result three instances of the self-renouncing attitude 'that Christ Jesus had' are set forth in the latter part of the chapter: (a) Paul himself, (b) Timothy for his unselfish service in the gospel and genuine concern for the Philippians, and finally (c) Epaphroditus whose devotion to his commission in the service of Christ was almost at the expense of his life.

In chap. 3:15 Paul encourages his dear friends at Philippi in their progress as Christians. He recognizes that not all of them have the same attitude of mind (φρονέω/*phroneō*) he has just mentioned, namely, of being filled with the burning ambition of fully gaining Christ. He presents himself as an example, not in any arrogant way for he knows what it is to struggle against difficulties, and paints the picture of a runner who presses on determinedly, aiming to finish the race and win the prize (vv. 12-14). He then effectively applies these words to the Philippians' lives for he wants them to be equally determined to fulfil the same ultimate aim that he has. He is an example in orientation and attitude as well as in his behaviour (v. 16).

The apostle calls upon the Philippians to be united in imitating his own example and that of others like him (Phil 3:17). In this context the apostolic model (τύπος/*typos*) is intended to stand over against and in stark contrast to those false examples of Christian behaviour in which there was a deliberate repudiation of all that the cross of Christ stood for (v. 18). Paul had warned the Philippians about these false Christians on a number of occasions previously and he does so again because of the potential threat they were to the congregations where they were active. The issues are momentous since they have to do with a person's ultimate destiny—either eternal destruction (v. 18) or a commonwealth in heaven (vv. 19, 20). Paul and his colleagues' example is thus intended to reinforce the serious warning not to be influenced by the enemies of the cross of Christ. It thus functions to reinforce Paul's call to perseverance which was clearly spelled out in 1:27-30.

At the conclusion of his final exhortations (Phil 4:1-9) the apostle urges his converts to live by the teaching and example he has given to them (v. 9). Using terms that were known in popular moral philosophy, he lists several positive ethical qualities ('whatever is true, noble, just', etc., v. 8), then summarizes them and describes comprehensively the characteristics that they are to reflect upon in order to shape their conduct ('yes, whatever is morally excellent [ἀρετή/aretē], whatever is praiseworthy [ἔπαινος/epainos]—let your thoughts continually dwell on these things [so that your conduct will be shaped by them]').

Paul wants to reinforce most vividly the points that he has made in his exhortations. These admonitions of vv. 2-9 are only loosely related to one another; however, they appear in the paragraph headed by the exhortation to 'stand firm' (στήκετε/stēkete, v. 1; cf. 1:27), and this is itself a repetition of his call to perseverance in 1:27-30. That call to stand firm is an essential element in the comprehensive injunction for the readers to 'live [their lives] in a manner worthy of the gospel of Christ' (1:27). So in chap. 4, as Paul addresses his dear friends with some of the most affectionate and endearing terms he ever uses in his letters ('My beloved brothers, whom I long for greatly, my joy and crown', v. 1) and concludes his exhortations (vv. 1-9), he uses himself as a model to reinforce the points of the admonitions in a vivid way and therefore to remind them of what constitutes a life worthy of the gospel of Christ.

To sum up. The apostle's example to his Christian friends at Philippi serves to underscore the *central* exhortation of the letter ('Now, the important thing is this: live as citizens of heaven in a manner that is worthy of the gospel of Christ', 1:27), an injunction which is part of the leading proposition that they should stand firm in the gospel (1:27-30). However, given the close connection between the apostle's life-style and the gospel he proclaims (cf. 1:12-26), is there more to Paul's being a pattern than this?

(b) Paul as a Model to the Thessalonians

In the first chapter of 1 Thessalonians the apostle does not call on his readers to imitate him; instead, he points out that they have already been doing so.[8] He praises them for following his and the

---

8   Cf. E. Best, *Paul and his Converts* (Edinburgh: Clark, 1988), 59-72, esp. 63.

Lord's example ('You *became* imitators of us and the Lord', 1 Thess 1:6; though cf. 2 Thess 3:7-9). Thus, Paul's Christian friends had joined him not only in suffering but also in love and the giving of themselves to others. A. J. Malherbe has rightly shown that, whenever Paul presents himself as a model to be emulated, he makes a close connection between his own life and the gospel. His behaviour and personal example could not finally be distinguished from the message he preached: his life authenticated the gospel (cf. 1 Thess 2:1-12).[9] This is not to suggest that he was seeking to make disciples for himself (2 Cor 4:5, 'We do not preach ourselves but Jesus as Lord, with ourselves as your slaves for the sake of Jesus'). But, as he sought to shape the community at Thessalonica within the context of a special relationship, Paul, who was an example in suffering, love and pastoral care (1 Thess 1-2), 'struggled as he gave himself to the preaching of the gospel for the benefit of others'.[10]

We agree with Malherbe's contention, and the earlier claims of J. H. Schütz,[11] that there is a particularly close relationship between the apostle's own life-style and the gospel he preaches. But this is not to imply that the living of a godly life is the same thing as proclaiming the saving message of Christ's death and resurrection. One ought not to confuse the content of the gospel with a manner of life lived in conformity with it. However, the close conjunction between the two forces us to reiterate the question more sharply: For what purposes is Paul a model to his converts?

A Commitment to the Spread of the Gospel?

Have we understood all that is involved in Paul's presentation of himself as a pattern to be followed? Did the apostle also expect his converts to be committed to the spread of the gospel as he was (though perhaps in rather different ways) so that others might be saved? Does his exhortation to imitate him include an admonition to evangelism and mission?

---

9   A. J. Malherbe, *Paul*, 54, 68. Cf. D. M. Stanley, 'Imitation in Paul's Letters: Its Significance for His Relationship to Jesus and to His Own Christian Foundations', *From Jesus to Paul. Studies in Honour of Francis Wright Beare*, ed. P. Richardson and J. C. Hurd (Waterloo, Ontario: Wilfred Laurier University, 1984), 127.

10   A. J. Malherbe, *Paul*, 54.

11   J. H. Schütz, *Paul*, 35-53.

The notion that the apostle expected Christians in his churches to be engaged in evangelistic outreach has not been acceptable to a range of scholars for a variety of reasons. Two recent writers may be taken as representative. The first is the missionary theologian, David Bosch, whose recent book, *Transforming Mission. Paradigm Shifts in Theology of Mission*, is an important and comprehensive contribution to current missiological debates.[12] In his treatment of the theme of mission in Paul, Bosch claims that the apostle expected believers to practice 'a missionary lifestyle' so that their behaviour would be exemplary and winsome, and that they would draw outsiders to the church like a powerful magnet. However, for Paul the 'primary responsibility of "ordinary" Christians is not to go out and preach, but to support the mission project through their appealing conduct and by making "outsiders" feel welcome in their midst'.[13]

The second is Paul Bowers who concluded, as part of a wider examination into Paul's understanding of his mission, that '*an energetic, mobile missionary initiative of the sort prosecuted by Paul himself is not described, expected, or enjoined for his churches*'.[14] This unexpected conclusion is not because 'Paul opposed churches becoming involved in active independent mission'. Rather, 'a concept of the church at mission failed to take any distinct shape in Paul's thinking'.[15] We shall turn to Bowers' broader treatment in the next chapter. For the present our particular concern is with his handling of 1 Corinthians 10:33–11:1 in which he concludes that Paul is not a model for 'evangelistic outreach to unbelievers' but for 'voluntary renunciation within the life of the community of one's rights in Christ'.[16]

Following Paul's Example as He Follows Christ

[9:19] Though I am free and belong to no man, I make myself a slave to everyone, to win as many as possible. [20] To the Jews I became like a Jew, to win the Jews. To those under the law I

---

12   New York: Orbis, 1991.

13   D. J. Bosch, *Transforming Mission*, 138.

14   W. P. Bowers, *Studies*, 119 (emphasis added). Cf. his recent article, 'Church and Mission in Paul', *JSNT* 44 (1991), 107.

15   W. P. Bowers, *Studies*, 120.

16   W. P. Bowers, *Studies*, 108; cf. his 'Church and Mission', 92-95.

became like one under the law (though I myself am not under the law), so as to win those under the law. [21] To those not having the law I became like one not having the law (though I am not free from God's law but am under Christ's law), so as to win those not having the law. [22] To the weak I became weak, to win the weak. I have become all things to all men so that by all possible means I might save some. [23] I do all this for the sake of the gospel, that I may share in its blessings. [10:31] So whether you eat or drink or whatever you do, do it all for the glory of God. [32] Do not cause anyone to stumble, whether Jews, Greeks or the church of God— [33] even as I try to please everybody in every way. For I am not seeking my own good but the good of many, so that they may be saved. [11:1] Follow my example, as I follow the example of Christ.

Before coming to any definite answer to this question as to whether the apostle expected his converts to be committed to the spread of the gospel as he was, on the grounds that this was intimately bound up with his modelling the kerygma, it is necessary to examine closely his admonition of the Corinthians at 1 Corinthians 11:1, 'Follow my example as I follow the example of Christ'.

At the conclusion of his long argument in 1 Corinthians 8-10 Paul offers himself as a paradigm for the kind of conduct that he has been urging on the Corinthians. He calls upon them to be imitators of himself as he is of Christ (11:1). In the immediately preceding verses Paul presented two comprehensive exhortations to the Corinthians: first, everything must be done to the glory of God (v. 31), and, secondly, they must give no offence to anyone—Jew, pagan or fellow-believer (v. 32). In these latter words it is generally agreed that the apostle is deliberately picking up what he has said in 9:19-23 about behaviour in relation to Jews, Gentiles and Christians. He then adds that he seeks not his own good but that of others so that they may be saved (ἵνα σωθῶσιν/*hina sōthōsin*, v. 33).

Many interpreters gloss over this final purpose clause or give it very little significance. However, one is forced to question whether this goal of Paul's, namely, his seeking the good of others so that Jews, Gentiles and 'weak' Christians may be saved, should be the Corinthians' objective as well, thereby serving as a motivating factor in their behaviour. It is generally recognized that Paul is instructing his readers to be imitators of him (and ultimately of

Christ) so that they will (1) do everything to the glory of God, and (2) give no offence to Jews, Gentiles and Christians. But is he also urging them (3) to seek the good of the many *in order that they may be saved*?

Because 1 Corinthians 8:1–11:1 is a unity and the language of 10:32 deliberately picks up what has been said in 9:19-23 in relation to Jews, Gentiles and 'weak' Christians, it is important to examine in detail Paul's statement about his missionary stance (9:19-23) before directing our attention to 10:31–11:1.

(a) Paul's servanthood and its goals (9:19-23).

These words in 9:19-23 are an expression of the stance which characterized Paul's whole missionary career. Although he is speaking about his own behaviour in a variety of situations, because of his total gospel orientation (vv. 12, 14, 16, 18, 23; cf. v. 25) one is forced to question whether he expects the Corinthians to adopt a similar line, even though the same divine necessity (ἀνάγκη/*anankē*) to preach the gospel has not been laid upon them (vv. 16-17).

In this paragraph Paul gives a defence of his social behaviour which differed according to the setting in which he found himself (whether Jewish or Gentile). His goal was to become all things to all people so that he might win as many as possible. These verses form part of a lengthy defence by Paul of his apostolic authority, and especially his apostolic freedom (9:1-27).

Traditionally it has been claimed that Paul is responding to an internal difficulty within the church at Corinth between the 'weak' and the 'strong' Christians over the question of marketplace food. But Gordon Fee has recently challenged this consensus: he argues that 'the vigorous, combative nature of Paul's answer . . . is scarcely the kind of response one would expect if [the Corinthians] had simply presented an internal question on which they had asked him to render a decision'. In fact, it is another issue to which Paul is responding, viz. not the eating of marketplace food but 'the eating of sacrificial food at the cultic meals in the pagan temples'.[17]

---

17   G. D. Fee, *The First Epistle to the Corinthians* (Grand Rapids: Eerdmans, 1987), 359; note his earlier advocacy of this in 'Ειδωλόθυτα Once Again: An Interpretation of 1 Corinthians 8-10', *Bib* 61 (1980), 172-197.

In a context where he makes a forthright statement about the divine compulsion under which he stands, Paul speaks about his apostolic restraint (vv. 15-18). He is under divine 'necessity' (ἀνάγκη/*anangkē*, v. 16), and thus cannot boast about his preaching the gospel to Gentiles. He chooses to proclaim this saving message 'free of charge', thereby not making use of his right to live by the gospel (v. 14). His great desire, described as his 'boast' (v. 16), is to do nothing that would in any way hinder the gospel (v. 12). Fee makes the further point: 'In offering the "free" gospel "free of charge" his own ministry becomes a living paradigm of the gospel itself'.[18]

As we turn to this passage closely we note the following important issues:

1. Paul's position or status—he is 'free' in Christ

Four times throughout the paragraph the apostle spells out his position or status which forms the basis for his conduct. He speaks of himself 'as being free' (v. 19), 'as not under the law' (v. 20), 'as not without law toward God', 'but under the law of Christ' (v. 21). Most interpreters agree that these four clauses are concessive ('Though I am free', etc.; cf. NIV, RSV, JB) with the expressions indicating Paul's freedom from the law, especially in matters of Jewish (religious) legal requirements.[19]

Paul's words of v. 20, 'I am not under the law', have particular reference to food offered to idols.[20] Jews, Gentile God-fearers or proselytes might abstain from eating such food because they were

---

18   G. D. Fee, *1 Corinthians*, 421.

19   G. Bornkamm, 'The Missionary Stance of Paul in 1 Corinthians 9 and in Acts', in *Studies in Luke-Acts*, ed. L. E. Keck and J. L. Martyn (London: SPCK, 1968), 194-207, esp. 195, claims that the concessive clause points to 'ultimate contrasts of a religious nature'. G. D. Fee, *1 Corinthians*, 425-426, esp. nn. 18, 20, understands Paul as referring to his financial independence from the Corinthians, not to an inner freedom, a freedom from sin or the law. But there are difficulties in the way of Fee's interpretation, not least of all because of the apostle's deliberate return in v. 19 to the issues of vv. 1-3 where 'freedom' is something broader than financial independence. Cf. D. B. Martin, *Slavery as Salvation. The Metaphor of Slavery in Pauline Christianity* (New Haven: Yale University, 1990), 69, who argues that throughout 1 Corinthians 9: 'The primary issue . . . is not simply Paul's freedom or apostleship but the connection of that freedom to his means of self-support by manual labor'.

20   C. K. Barrett, *A Commentary on the First Epistle to the Corinthians* (London: Black, 1968), 211, argues that 'Paul was prepared to abandon [the law] altogether'. Cf. P. Richardson, 'Pauline Inconsistency: 1 Corinthians 9.19-23 and Galatians 2.11-14', *NTS* 26 (1979-80), 347-362, esp. 347.

'under the law'. The issue for them was a matter of religious obligation. But Paul was not under the law in this sense. He was free and if he chose to abstain from eating it was because of his great desire to win those under the law for Christ (v. 20; cf. v. 12b).

On the other hand, the apostle is not 'lawless' (ἄνομος/*anomos*, v. 21), in the sense of godless or wicked (cf. 1 Tim 1:9). Quite the reverse. And to avoid any misunderstanding, he makes the point plain by adding in v. 21 a further clause by way of explanation: he is 'under the law of Christ' (ἔννομος Χριστοῦ/*ennomos Christou*, v. 21).[21] Paul is bound not only to the body of ordinances or demands given by Jesus but also 'by all that Christ accomplished and represents'.[22]

His position, then, which forms the background for his accommodating behaviour in different social settings is that of one who is truly 'free' in Christ. He is not under the law in the sense that he is obliged to keep Jewish legal requirements in relation to food. Yet he is not lawless or godless since he stands under the rule of Christ, that is, his teachings and all that he has accomplished and represents. While it was in his encounter with the risen Christ on the Damascus road that Paul was compelled to preach the gospel (v. 16), the basis for his flexible conduct in different settings lay in *his freedom in Christ*; that is, it was grounded in his being a Christian, not in his apostleship as such. This will provide, in part at least, the basis for the injunction that he will lay on the Corinthians at the end of the long section (8:1–11:1).

2. His goal—the salvation of men and women

In this well-rounded passage Paul not only sets forth the position which forms the background to his conduct. He also indicates what his aims or goals are as he adopts certain stances. Seven times over in the space of five verses he concludes with a purpose construction (ἵνα/*hina*, 'in order that').[23] The first five sentences employ the missionary term κερδαίνω/*kerdainō* ('gain', 'win'): Paul aims to 'win' the many, that is, Jews, those under the law, those not under law and weak Christians. In the general sentence of v. 22 he

---

21   This unusual expression is probably related to 'the law of Christ' in Galatians 6:2.

22   D. A. Carson, 'Pauline Inconsistency: Reflections on 1 Corinthians 9.19-23 and Galatians 2.11-14', *Churchman* 100 (1986), 12. Note the additional bibliographical details.

23   When the paragraph is read aloud these clauses sound rather monotonous.

uses the more common synonym σώζω/*sōzō* ('save'), while in v. 23
he states that the two fold reason for doing all this is: (1) for the
sake of the gospel, and (2) *in order that* (lit.) 'I might become a
fellow-participant in it'. Paul's apparently inconsistent behaviour in
a variety of social settings has basically one goal—the salvation of
others.

The verb 'to win' (κερδαίνω/*kerdainō*), which is used five times
in these verses, was a well known missionary term[24] and here it has
been taken to refer to Paul's goal of *converting* 'as many as possible'
(v. 19), including Jews and Gentiles (vv. 20-21). However, it
cannot refer exclusively to their conversion since in v. 22 he speaks
of his aim of winning 'the weak', a designation which should be
understood of Christians (rather than non-Christians; cf. Rom 5:6),
whose consciences trouble them about matters which are not in
themselves wrong (cf. 1 Cor 8). Paul's goal of winning Jews,
Gentiles and weak Christians has to do with their full maturity in
Christ and thus signifies *winning them completely*. To win Gentiles
does not describe simply a goal of converting them, though this, of
course, is included. It has, rather, to do with his ultimate purpose
for them, namely, their being brought to perfection in Christ on
the final day. Nothing short of this will fulfil Paul's ambitions for
them. Similarly, his goal of winning 'weak' Christians has to do
with their full maturity and blamelessness at the second coming.
On this interpretation κερδαίνω/*kerdainō* has a consistent meaning
throughout the paragraph.[25]

Further, the parallel verb 'to save' (v. 22), which usually has a
future orientation in Paul's letters, is best understood as meaning 'to
save from the coming wrath on the final day', and so 'to save
[completely]', not simply 'to convert'. 'Win' or 'save' then speaks
not only of the initial activity whereby a person comes to faith, but
of the whole process by which a Jew, a Gentile or a weak Christian
is brought to glory. This approach is in line with our earlier

---

24   D. Daube, *The New Testament and Rabbinic Judaism* (London: Athlone, 1956), 352-361,
     has shown that its Hebrew equivalent had already been taken over into Judaism as
     missionary language.

25   D. A. Carson, 'Pauline Inconsistency', 14 (following D. Daube, *Rabbinic Judaism*, 352-
     361), argues somewhat differently that 'the verb can refer both to winning someone
     from paganism or Judaism to Christianity, and to winning someone from faltering or
     inadequate Christianity to a more robust faith'. On this view, the verb has different
     nuances in vv. 20-21 and v. 22, while in v. 19 'win' must cover both connotations.

conclusions that when Paul speaks of preaching the gospel (εὐαγγελίζομαι/*euangelizomai*), he can include a range of activities from the initial proclamation of the kerygma to the building up of believers and grounding them firmly in the faith. His concerns are to evangelize men and women, and to form them into well-established Christian communities. This understanding of the apostle's words harmonizes with his statements elsewhere in which he anticipates his converts being his joy and crown as they stand fast on the final day, demonstrating that he has not run in vain in his ministry (2 Cor 1:14; Gal 2:2; Phil 2:16; 4:1; 1 Thess 2:19).

Finally, the enigmatic v. 23 makes sense on this view of Paul's ultimate goal. His flexibility shown in a variety of social settings is 'for the sake of the gospel' and '*in order that* (lit.) 'I might become a fellow-participant in it'. This final purpose clause does not mean that Paul's salvation is in doubt because it is dependent on the success of his apostolic ministry.[26] Instead, the clause could refer to his sharing with others in the benefits, that is, the blessings and promises, of the gospel.[27] However, a stronger case has been made, in our view, on grounds of word usage, grammar and context for understanding this clause of Paul's participation in the gospel's dynamic progress.[28] He is the gospel's fellow-sharer or partner.[29] 'His missionary activity takes place in the shadow of the energetic working of the gospel itself'.[30] He has renounced his apostolic rights because of his determination not to place any obstacles in the way of the gospel's effective working (v. 12b). Paul 'has done all this to become [a] participant in the dynamic character of the gospel—to share in the gospel's *own*

---

26 Against A. Satake, 'Apostolat', 96-103. Note the critique of S. Kim, *Origin*, 288-296, and the recent detailed argument of J. M. Gundry Volf, *Paul and Perseverance* (Tübingen: Mohr, 1990), 247-254.

27 So G. D. Fee, *1 Corinthians*, 432, summarizing the views of others.

28 J. H. Schütz, *Paul*, 51-52, and J. M. Gundry Volf, *Paul*, 247-254.

29 The genitive case αὐτοῦ/*autou* ('of him/it') with συγκοινωνός/*sunkoinōnos* ('sharer', partner') can refer to the *person* with whom one takes part. Cf. BDF, para. 182(1). Accordingly, the αὐτοῦ/*autou* points to *the gospel* (as personified) with whom Paul participates. Note Phil 1:7.

30 J. M. Gundry Volf, *Paul*, 251.

31 J. H. Schütz, *Paul*, 51-52. He adds: '"To share in the gospel" and "to win men" are two ways of saying the same thing. And it is this dynamic or "pregnant" use of the gospel—the gospel as itself an effective force or agent—with which Paul works here'.

32 J. M. Gundry Volf, *Paul*, 253; cf. E. Molland, *Euangelion*, 54.

work'.[31] His 'aim is to become the gospel's partner . . . in bringing people into the sphere of salvation'.[32]

3. The wide range of contexts in which Paul serves as a slave

The third element of significance in this paragraph where Paul speaks of his freedom to act is the different social settings in which he finds himself. The opening verse (v. 19) presupposes a range of varying contexts, while vv. 20-22 proceed to spell out four of these.

The first setting Paul draws to the Corinthians' attention is a Jewish one where obviously questions of Jewish law were at stake (v. 20). It has been argued that because of the parallels with 10:23-33 food laws are the specific issue here, particularly 'the prohibition against eating marketplace food because of its associations with idolatry'.[33] As indicated above, this suggestion makes good sense. But Paul does not specifically restrict his statements to food laws, which he could easily have done. He is apparently keen to describe his stance in rather more general terms ('to the Jews I became as a Jew'), suggesting that while his voluntary renunciation had to do with food laws at Corinth, it might involve the laying aside of other rights in relation to Jews elsewhere. What the apostle had to say was particularly relevant at Corinth; but that was not the only place where he would behave 'as a Jew' in order to win Jews. In another context becoming 'like a Jew' might have involved some flexibility in relation to circumcision (1 Cor 7:19; Gal 6:15), as in the case of Timothy (Acts 16:1-3), or the observance of special days[34] (cf. Col 2:16).

In the latter half of v. 20 Paul varies his language slightly to describe the second setting: 'to those under the law I became like one under the law'. This might be intended to include Gentile God-fearers and proselytes, along with natural born Jews.[35] But even if this distinction is correct, the social setting Paul has in view

---

33 So G. D. Fee, *1 Corinthians*, 428.

34 It appears from the Book of Acts that Paul arranged his visits to Jerusalem around the major Jewish festivals (cf. 20:16).

35 Cf. H. L. Ellison, 'Paul and the Law—"All Things to All Men"', in *Apostolic History and the Gospel. Biblical and Historical Essays Presented to F. F. Bruce*, ed. W. W. Gasque and R. P. Martin (Exeter: Paternoster, 1970), 195-202, esp. 196, and G. D. Fee, *1 Corinthians*, 429, n. 39.

is parallel to the first, that is, a Jewish context, even if the emphasis is now on the law or questions of Jewish legal requirements.

The third setting in which Paul serves as a slave concerns 'those not having the law' (v. 21). Clearly, this had special reference to his calling as an apostle to the Gentiles[36] and included the majority of the Corinthian believers who had been Gentile converts.

One might have thought that by referring to the categories of Jews and Gentiles, or those under the law and those outside it, the apostle had in fact referred to everyone in the Roman empire![37] But there was another group of people with whom he related and thus a different context in which he might serve as a slave (v. 19): 'to the weak', that is, the majority of the Corinthian believers (cf. 1:26-31), he 'became weak' in order to win them (v. 22). Together these four categories make up the 'everyone' of v. 19 and the 'all [people]' of v. 22.

What is most interesting in this paragraph is the wide, indeed universal, range of settings in which the apostle is prepared to serve as a slave for the sake of the gospel. He is willing to work among Jews, Gentiles and weak Christians. Although he is here referring to specific social settings, particularly those relating to eating marketplace food with its idolatrous associations, his remarks do not necessarily mean they had to be restricted to these social contexts. Though specifically applicable to the Corinthian situation, they seem to allow a broader application. Paul refers to a stance adopted in relation to the problems at Corinth. But his language suggests that he is able to behave freely and appropriately in relation to Jews, Gentiles and weak Christians *elsewhere*. He appears to be talking about a specific series of stances he has taken which are consistent with a carefully thought out policy in relation to the gospel. This is why his words are so timely for Christians generally. G. Bornkamm's observations about this are correct,[38] and those commentators who so contextualize and limit the apostle's statements to the Corinthian scene, as though this was a 'one off' stance, have failed to come to grips with his actual wording.

---

36   See below for a discussion of Paul's earnest desire, as one who had an important role to play in salvation historical purpose of God for *Gentiles*, to 'win Jews'.

37   There were, of course, other categories that could have been used to describe humanity, but this was certainly one way, albeit along salvation historical lines, of speaking of everyone.

38   G. Bornkamm, 'Missionary Stance', 194-207.

The fact that Paul is prepared to work among Jews, Gentiles and weak Christians 'in order to win as many as possible' is all the more significant given that he was called to be an apostle to the Gentiles. Of course, it might be countered that in the nature of the case he would necessarily come across Jews as he sought to evangelize Gentiles, especially if his initial approach was to reach God-fearers in the synagogue (cf. Acts 13:5, 14; 14:1, etc.). Paul adopted a wise pragmatic policy, the argument runs.

But the issue is more fundamental than this. In the salvation historical plan of God it was necessary for the gospel to be preached first to Jews and then to Gentiles. This divine priority had been sanctioned in the promises given to Abraham (Gen 12:1-3), and reiterated on a number of occasions in both testaments (note esp. Isa 49:6; Rom 1:16-17; cf. Acts 13:46-48). Paul's strong conviction that he had been called by God 'to preach [his Son] among the Gentiles' (Gal 1:16; cf. Rom 15:16; Eph 3:8) in no way interfered with that divine plan. Quite the reverse. According to Romans 9-11 the apostle's missionary task was wholly consistent with those divine purposes in which God would have mercy on Jew and Gentile alike (Rom 11:32). Indeed, he desired through his ministry to Gentiles to arouse his own people to envy and save some of them (11:14).

Thus, Paul's calling as an important figure in God's plan of salvation is not to be understood in a restrictive or limiting sense, as though he was allowed to preach the gospel only to Gentiles. It was his practice to preach to Jews in synagogues since he earnestly desired that they might be saved (Rom 10:1). Paul would do nothing to cause them any unnecessary offense (1 Cor 10:32-33) and he was prepared, if it were possible, to be cursed and separated from Christ eternally for the sake of his Jewish brothers and sisters (Rom 9:2, 3).

4. His overall stance—he makes himself a slave

Finally, the apostle spells out his overall posture and the particular line he adopts, as a concrete expression of that stance, in the different social settings. Of cardinal importance is his opening statement where he uses the language of servanthood to refer to his *overall* stance: Paul *makes himself a slave* (ἐδούλωσα/*edoulōsa*) to everyone for the purpose of winning as many as possible (v. 19). This language is highly significant and assumes a prominent role within Paul's argument in these chapters (8:1–11:1): his words are picked up at the end of the long treatment in 10:31–11:1 where they serve an important function within his concluding exhortations.

For Paul Jesus is the supreme example of humble, self-sacrificing, self-giving service. He emptied himself by taking 'the form of a slave (δοῦλος/*doulos*)' and humbled himself by becoming obedient to the utmost limit, death on the cross. Jesus is the 'Lordly Example' (cf. Phil 2:5-8),[39] to use L. W. Hurtado's phrase, and the paradigm of servanthood and of true Christian ministry. His humble, self-giving service is set before the Philippians as Paul urges them to show unity and humility in their relations with one another (cf. 2:1-4). The apostle regularly uses servant language to describe his own ministry (δοῦλοι/*douloi*, 2 Cor 4:5) and to express believers' relationships with one another (δουλεύετε/*douleuete*, Gal 5:13).[40] The radical nature of these expressions can hardly be overestimated. Slavery in contemporary society pointed to the extreme deprivation of one's rights, including those relating to one's own life and person. When Jesus emptied himself by embracing the divine vocation and becoming incarnate he became a slave, without any rights whatever (Phil 2:7). He displayed the nature or form of God in the nature or form of a slave, therefore showing clearly not only what his character was like, but also what it meant to be God.

As one who was 'free' but who voluntarily *made himself* a slave, Paul was living in conformity with the example of his Lord and thus showing a truly Christian life-style. The Corinthians had believed that their apostle was second-rate (vv. 15-18) and that he was guilty of vacillating and inconsistent behaviour. They could not have been further from the truth, for he had willingly renounced his rights and put himself at the disposal of others. Later

---

39   For a detailed examination of this paragraph, including its function within the immediate context of Phil 1:27–2:18 and the letter as a whole, see P. T. O'Brien, *Philippians*, 186-271.

40   Rightly noted by G. D. Fee, *1 Corinthians*, 426. For a recent sociological examination of slavery in 1 Corinthians, see D. B. Martin, *Slavery as Salvation*.

41   In the first sentence (v. 20) which gives a clue to understanding the others the καί/*kai* has been regarded as epexegetic; so A. Robertson and A. Plummer, *A Critical and Exegetical Commentary on the First Epistle of St Paul to the Corinthians* (Edinburgh: Clark, ²1914), 191, and G. D. Fee, *1 Corinthians*, 427, n. 27.

he will call upon them to follow his example as he follows the pattern of Christ (11:1).

What Paul's overall stance of making himself a slave involved[41] in the different social contexts is spelled out in vv. 20-22. First, in a setting where he sought to win Jews Paul 'became *like* a Jew'. This is a surprising statement, for he was already a Jew by birth and upbringing. When later he writes to the Philippians and spells out his orthodox Jewish pedigree and upbringing (Phil 3:5), although his attitude to these inherited privileges underwent a revolution when he came to a knowledge of Christ Jesus his Lord (vv. 7, 8), in some senses he did not cease to be a Jew: he was still one who had been circumcised on the eighth day, a member of the nation of Israel, belonging to the tribe of Benjamin and a Hebrew of Hebrews (cf. 2 Cor 11:22, 'Are they Hebrews? So *am* I. Are they Israelites? So *am* I'). Having been born into the chosen race of Israelite parents and subsequently circumcised, Paul inherited all the privileges of the covenant community, privileges he enumerates in relation to Israel, even after his conversion, at Romans 9:4-5: 'Theirs is the adoption as sons, theirs the divine glory, the covenants, the receiving of the law, the temple worship and the promises. Theirs are the patriarchs, and from them is traced the human ancestry of Christ who is God over all, forever praised!'

But in another sense Paul must have stopped being a Jew, for how else could he have become '*like* a Jew'? The matters in view here were regulations and ceremonies which Jews regarded as essential to a right relationship with God, but which Paul had given up when he became a Christian.[42] These presumably included circumcision (1 Cor 7:19; Gal 6:15), food laws (1 Cor 8:8; Gal 2:10-13; Rom 14:17; Col 2:16) and the observance of special days (Col 2:16).[43] In themselves, they were religiously indifferent and Paul was free to observe them or not. But he hotly opposed anyone who required them of Gentile converts because they considered these provided (or maintained) a right relationship with God.[44] They were not forbidden, however, to the Christian and Paul was prepared to follow Jewish ways when in Jewish company. So his willingness to take part, on his last visit to Jerusalem, in the

---

42   Cf. F. F. Bruce, *1 and 2 Corinthians*, 86.

43   G. D. Fee, *1 Corinthians*, 428.

44   Cf. H. Conzelmann, *I Corinthians* (Philadelphia: Fortress, 1975), 160.

discharge of a Nazirite vow in the temple (Acts 21:23ff.) is consistent with this statement of his policy.

The following clause (v. 20b), 'to those under the law I became *like* one under the law (though I myself am not under the law)', is parallel with the preceding and gives us a further clue as to its meaning. The 'law' here is the Jewish law, with its 613 written precepts of the Pentateuch, and probably also includes the 'oral law' or 'tradition of the elders' which amplified the meaning of the written precepts. Paul abstained from eating when in the company of those under the law in order that he might win them; they abstained, however, as a matter of religious obligation.

On the other hand, in the company of Gentiles Paul 'made himself a slave' by eating 'whatever was put before him without raising questions of conscience' (10:27). It is not suggested that Gentiles had no sense of any kind of law (cf. Rom 2:14); only that they were 'outside the scope of the Jewish law' (cf. NEB).

While the first three stances which Paul adopts—as expressions of his making himself a slave to all—have to do with Jewish or Gentile social settings, the final position he takes up is in relation to weak Christians: 'to the weak I became weak' (v. 22). These may well have been those with whom Paul was in dispute within the church, that is, Christians whose consciences troubled them about matters which were not in themselves wrong (1 Cor 8:13-9:1). On the other hand, the expression may be used more generally to describe the majority of the Corinthian Christians (cf. 1:26-31) and that Paul is speaking of becoming weak (cf. 4:9-13) for this was a paradigm of the Christian life.

The final words of v. 22 summarize the earlier examples: 'I have become all things to all people [so that by all possible means I might save some]'. Although Paul was charged with being inconsistent in relation to eating 'kosher' food, and therefore he had no right to forbid the Corinthians from eating sacrificial food at cultic meals in pagan temples, it is clear that his behaviour demonstrated a higher consistency than his opponents understood. It was the outworking of his deep concern for the progress of the

---

45   The imperatives of vv. 31-32, which are joined to what precedes by the inferential 'therefore' (οὖν/*oun*), wrap up Paul's long argument of chaps. 8-10. Note the helpful exegesis of this paragraph by G. Fee, *1 Corinthians*, 487-490, to whom I am indebted.

gospel and the saving of men and women—Jews, Gentiles and weak Christians (cf. 10:32-33).

(b) Paul's servanthood as a model (10:31–11:1).

At the conclusion of his long argument in chaps. 8-10 (esp. 10:23–11:1)[45] Paul offers himself as a paradigm for the kind of conduct he has been urging on the Corinthians (cf. 4:15-17).[46] As we have seen, he appeals to his own example and exhorts them to imitate himself in the same way that he has 'imitated' his Lord: 'Follow my example, as I follow the example of Christ' (11:1). In calling on the Corinthians to do this Paul has in mind the model he has already set before them in his earlier 'defence' (9:19-23; cf. 4:15-17). There he stated that he had voluntarily made himself a slave (ἐδούλωσα/*edoulōsa*, 9:19). He had conformed to the example of his Master by willingly renouncing his rights and putting himself at the disposal of others (cf. Phil 2:7). Now he wants the Corinthians to follow this dominical and apostolic model.

But what, in fact, does Paul actually expect of the Corinthians when he offers himself as a model to them? Although the 'presenting problem' among them has been the issue of eating food at cultic meals in pagan temples, the apostle lays two *comprehensive exhortations* on them. He clearly expects a changed attitude and right behaviour in relation to these cultic meals. But his admonitions are not limited to the specifics. Paul broadens the perspective so that the Corinthians' whole life-style is to be lived to God's honour and praise. Hence, the admonition, 'do everything for the glory of God' (v. 31).

Secondly, they must give no offence to anyone—Jew, Gentile or fellow-believer (v. 32). This too is a wide-ranging injunction which comes under the rubric of conforming to Paul's model. To 'give offence' refers not so much to the Corinthians hurting someone's feelings as to preventing them from hearing the gospel or causing them to stumble so that they do not believe it. The negative expression 'to give no offence' is now spelled out

---

46   'Paul's conduct remains the standard of the imperative to the Corinthians', D. A. Carson, 'Pauline Inconsistency', 15. Cf. W. P. De Boer, *Imitation*, 154-169.

47   This appears to be the significance of the 'even as' (καθώς/*kathōs*) here.

48   G. Fee, *1 Corinthians*, 490.

positively[47] (in terms similar to vv. 23–24) as Paul affirms 'I try to please everybody in every way'. This is a remarkable statement, for as G. Fee rightly notes, 'pleasing people' in the context of evangelism is 'otherwise anathema to Paul'[48] (1 Thess 2:4; Gal 1:10). Here, however, he has in view itinerant philosophers and charlatans who curried favour with others in order to win their hearers' approval. Paul wants the Corinthians to be motivated and concerned for the 'advantage' (σύμφερον/*sympheron*) of the many, which he then defines as 'so that they may be saved'.[49] Like him the readers are to seek 'the *advantage* of the many' and so be committed to their salvation as he was. This objective was a fundamental ingredient in the apostolic model he has provided and should be the Corinthians' goal as well as his own. He expects them to be involved in the progress of the gospel as he was. His ambitions should be theirs. They too should do everything 'for the sake of the gospel' since they are fellow-participants in its dynamic progress (9:23).

Conclusions: Committed to the Gospel and the Salvation of Others

The results of our exegesis of 10:31–11:1 are confirmed by what we observed in Paul's 'defence' of 9:19–23. In speaking about the stance that characterized his whole missionary career he focussed on four cardinal elements, the first three of which were applicable to the Corinthians.

(1) Paul's status or position from which he varied his behaviour in different social settings was his being 'free' in Christ (9:19). Although it was in his encounter with the risen Lord on the Damascus road that he was compelled to preach the gospel (v. 16), the basis for his flexible conduct in different settings lay in his *freedom in Christ* and his total gospel orientation. His behaviour was grounded in his being a Christian, not in his apostleship as such.

(2) Paul's overall stance of making himself a slave (ἐδούλωσα/*edoulōsa*, v. 19) was paradigmatic for the Corinthians. As one who was free, he was living in conformity with the example of his Lord and thus showing a truly Christian life-style. He

---

49   H. Conzelmann, *I Corinthians*, 179: 'The content of what is "advantageous" is defined by the ἵνα[*hina*]-clause: salvation'.

followed the servant model of his Master (cf. Phil 2:7); let them and other Christians do the same.

(3) The salvation of men and women was Paul's goal (1 Cor 9:19-23). His earnest desire was to win Jews, Gentiles and weak Christians, that is, to save them completely so that they would be pure and blameless at the second coming. The Corinthians' ambitions, and ours too, should be the same.

(4) We have seen that the apostle knew how to behave appropriately in a wide range of social settings: with Gentile God-fearers and proselytes, Jews and Gentiles, along with other Christians. Although his overall stance of making himself a slave (v. 19) was paradigmatic for the Corinthians, the actual outworking of this for his readers might vary. Paul is not suggesting that they should be engaged in the same wide-ranging, apostolic ministry in which he has been involved. He is neither offering practical counsel on how to live the life of an apostle nor suggesting that other Christians have the same calling and gifts that he has. Nor is his purpose to instruct church planters as to how to engage in their ministry. Rather, his aim is to 'enjoin all Christians to follow his example and refuse to stand on their rights if the well-being of their fellow-believers [and others] is called into jeopardy'.[50] But a commitment to the 'advantage' of many is a commitment to their salvation.

In the light of these exegetical and theological conclusions we return to the two representative writers who raised serious doubts as to whether Paul expected Christians in his churches to be engaged in evangelistic outreach.

(a) According to David Bosch, believers were urged by Paul to practice 'a missionary lifestyle' so that their behaviour would be exemplary and winsome. As a result they would draw outsiders to the church like a powerful magnet. However, it was not their primary responsibility to go out and preach. Instead, they were 'to support the mission project through their appealing conduct and by making "outsiders" feel welcome in their midst'.[51]

It is undoubtedly right to draw attention to Paul's concern for the Christians' godly lifestyle and exemplary behaviour (both for their own sake and the winsome effects they were likely to have on

---

50   D. A. Carson, 'Pauline Inconsistency', 16.

51   D. J. Bosch, *Transforming Mission*, 138.

outsiders). The conclusions reached in our study of Paul as a
model to the Philippians and to the Thessalonians have established
this. At the same time the apostle still expected his Christian
friends to be committed to the gospel just as he was. This is
implied in the Thessalonian correspondence and mentioned at
Philippi (see the following chapter). Our more detailed study of 1
Corinthians 8-10 has demonstrated that the Corinthians as
Christian men and women were to be committed to the gospel just
as Paul was. They too should do everything for its sake, for like
their apostle they were fellow-participants in its dynamic progress.
They were to seek 'the advantage of the many', that is, their
salvation (10:33). The Corinthians' ambitions were to be the same
as Paul's, their apostolic model. Bosch's *limitation of believers'
responsibility* to supporting the mission by their winsome lifestyle
fails to take account of the Pauline teaching about the dynamic of
the gospel, and the goal of saving others which the Corinthians are
to have in *everything they do* as a necessary element in following
Paul's example.

(b) Similarly, Paul Bowers' stress on the Corinthians' need
voluntarily to renounce their rights within the life of the
community is consistent with Paul's emphasis in the passage. But
the particular issue at stake in our discussion is whether there is an
additional nuance that takes into account the good of unbelievers,
and we have concluded on exegetical grounds that the Corinthians
are urged to have the same aims as Paul their example, and thus,
among other things, to be committed to the salvation of others.
Bowers in our judgment has failed to treat adequately the final
purpose clause of 1 Corinthians 10:33, 'so that they may be saved'.
His conclusions, therefore, are inadequate, and this is all the more
significant given that he has specifically raised the question about
the relationship between Paul's *understanding of his own mission* and
his theology of mission generally. It is at this point of Paul and the
Corinthians' commitment to and identification with the gospel that
the critical link between Paul's missionary task and that of his
fellow-Christians is made. The apostle may not have expected his
converts at Corinth to be engaged in missionary initiatives of the
kind he was furthering; but each *in his or her own way and according to
their personal gifts* was to have the same goal and ambitions as Paul
himself, that is, that of seeking by all possible means to save many.
They were to be consumed by passion as he was!

Paul called on his readers to follow his example as he followed that of Christ. He had made himself a slave as had Jesus Christ who had humbled himself to death; he had lived in conformity with this dominical model and thus showed a truly Christian lifestyle. The apostle's goal of *saving many* was an essential element in the servant pattern he adopted ('I have made myself a slave to all, so that I might win as many as possible') and should have been the Corinthians' objective as well as his own. He expected them, therefore, to be committed to evangelism just as he was. Paul's ambitions were to be theirs. And what is more they should be ours!

CHAPTER 5

THE PAULINE GREAT COMMISSION

Ephesians 6:10-20

The question has often been raised as to why so little is written in the Pauline letters about the need for Christians to evangelize. Is it because believers in Paul's churches were consistently speaking about Jesus as Lord to their non-Christian friends, and therefore did not need to be urged to do so? This is the view of many who consider that once Paul had founded and built up Christian communities, he expected that they might become centres of outreach for the gospel, with each congregation assuming responsibility for the evangelization of its own region. As soon as Paul's own task was complete and he had moved on, the apostolic mission would continue towards the goal of giving everyone an opportunity of hearing and believing the message of Jesus Christ, the crucified and risen Lord.

Michael Green is one who takes this line. He states: Paul 'seems to have made a point of setting up two or three centres of the faith in a province, and then passing on, and allowing the native enthusiasm and initiative of the converts to lead them to others whom they could win for Christ'.[1] Similarly, Ferdinand Hahn asserts: 'Paul was content on each occasion to carry the gospel to the centres of a district and to trust that the message would spread out from there'.[2] On this view, Paul's apparently extravagant claims

---

1   M. Green, *Evangelism in the early Church* (London: Hodder, 1970), 263. He adds: Paul's 'preaching had been representative; each province had heard something of the gospel, and little Christian communities were planted there to continue the work'.

2   F. Hahn, *Mission*, 16. Cf. G. Bornkamm, *Paul*, 54, who, among others claims that 'the gospel needed only to be preached for it to spread automatically'. He cited Harnack with approval: 'The presumption is that the fire [of the gospel] will of itself spread to the right and the left of where it was kindled'.

regarding the spread of the gospel (e.g. Col 1:23, 'the gospel that you heard, which has been proclaimed to every creature under heaven'; cf. Rom 1:8; 15:19; 1 Thess 1:8) might be read as statements of strategic rather than ultimate achievement.[3]

Although believers in several of the Pauline congregations seem to have been active in evangelizing their non-Christian friends, this does not appear to have been universally the case. Further, even when Christians demonstrated their obedience to other apostolic injunctions and Paul was genuinely pleased with their progress in the faith, he urges them to continue as they have begun. So, for example, the Thessalonians are commended for their 'brotherly love', and told that they do not need to be written to about the matter. Yet Paul urges them to show this Christian grace 'more and more' (1 Thess 4:9-10). Similarly, the Philippians are encouraged to 'hold fast to what they have attained' and to press on in the same direction (Phil 3:16). As a parallel, then, if the believers in the Pauline churches were actively engaged in evangelism, and the apostle was genuinely pleased with their commitment to the spread of the gospel, we might have expected him to urge them to continue in this important activity. But such is not the case, unless Paul is making the point in other, but apparently less obvious, ways. The conclusions of Green, Hahn and others about the early Christians being actively engaged in evangelism and mission have, therefore, been seriously questioned.

Churches as Ongoing Instruments of Mission?

How then do we explain this apparent paucity of references to the need for Christians to evangelize? The puzzle has been put another way: were the emerging churches which the apostle had founded meant in turn to focus upon ongoing mission themselves? Was it Paul's intention that each new congregation should assume a responsibility in its own area for completing the work which he had begun?

Paul Bowers, for one, thinks not. In a lengthy critical survey,[4] he examined three categories of material in Paul's letters which have

---

3   According to W. P. Bowers, 'Church and Mission', 90, this is a commonly held assumption, particularly with reference to Romans 15:19 (see chapter 2); cf. E. Best, G. Bornkamm, R. Bultmann, J. A. Grassi, M. Green, F. Hahn, D. Senior and C. Stuhlmueller, and J. Ziesler.

4   W. P. Bowers, *Studies*, 103-121, and his article, 'Church and Mission', 89-111.

been understood to support the view that the apostle regarded his churches as instruments of active ongoing mission: first, those passages in which he seems to expect his converts to engage in missionary outreach as a natural corollary of his own missionary commitments, or where he urges them to be imitators of his own life and practice, and the 'very exhortation to imitation includes implicitly an exhortation to mission'.[5] Secondly, Paul's concept of the church, especially where it appears to be experiencing a numerical increase that is being encouraged by its members.[6] Thirdly, those instances where Paul seems to represent various churches as engaged in missionary activity and he approves of it, e.g. 1 Thessalonians 1:8, 'For the word of the Lord has sounded forth from you not only in Macedonia and Achaia'.[7]

At the end of his lengthy evaluation Bowers concluded: 'we cannot speak of a definite concept unambiguously present in Paul of the church as an intended independent instrument of active mission'.[8] Even where the apostle thinks of the church as itself involved in something evangelistic, it is not an active outreach or deliberate mission on the Pauline model that is in view. The believers are to avoid giving offence (1 Cor 10:32–11:1), or their common life is noised abroad among unbelievers (1 Thess 1:8), or they are encouraged to take advantage of any inquiries (Col 4:5-6). But 'an energetic, mobile missionary initiative of the sort prosecuted by Paul himself is not described, expected [of], or enjoined . . . [on] his churches'.[9] However, Bowers later concedes that in the apostle's letters there are references to an active outreach for the spread of the gospel and the founding of new believing communities. This is not undertaken by churches *as* churches. Instead, it occurs through 'individual believers, alone or collectively, [who are] directed by God and assisted by church communities'.[10]

---

5   W. P. Bowers, *Studies*, 104. The relevant passages are: 1 Cor 4:16; 11:1; 2 Cor 5:18–6:2; Phil 3:17; 1 Thess 1:6-7; 2 Thess 3:7-9. See our treatment in chapter 4.

6   W. P. Bowers, *Studies*, 110-112, and 'Church and Mission', 95-97.

7   Rom 1:8; 2 Cor 3:2; Phil 2:15-16; Col 4:5; 1 Thess 1:8. Note W. P. Bowers, *Studies*, 112-118; 'Church and Mission', 97-101. In the latter Bowers comments that the 'sounding out' of the word of the Lord 'may then actually denote not the spreading gospel but instead the spreading report on the gospel's triumph at Thessalonica. The report of this event had become a word of encouragement, good news, to other churches' (99).

8   W. P. Bowers, *Studies*, 118-119.

9   W. P. Bowers, *Studies*, 119; 'Church and Mission', 107.

10   W. P. Bowers, 'Church and Mission', 107.

What, then, is Paul's understanding of the relationship between his churches and his ongoing mission? Bowers' response to this question is fivefold: (1) the churches themselves are the goal of his missionary activity. (2) They are encouraged to support his mission by prayer and financial help, thereby becoming partners with him in it. (3) By their attractive behaviour and positive response to inquiries they will encourage others to join their congregations. (4) They are to carry on Paul's nurturing work so that they and others will grow into Christian maturity. And (5) they are to maintain cordial relationships with other congregations founded by the Pauline mission.[11]

As a contribution to this debate we concluded in our third chapter (on Rom 1:1-17) that the dynamic of the gospel's logic meant for believers a deeper commitment to its ongoing, powerful advance, as well as to the person who was at its centre. Those who had truly experienced the saving power of the gospel in their own lives and had the assurance of deliverance from the wrath to come on the final day, could not be anything other than debtors to those for whom Christ died—just as Paul himself was a debtor. Knowing the desperate plight of men and women under divine judgment and that the gospel was the only hope for deliverance from the wrath to come, those who had once been in this predicament should be wholly involved in bringing it into the hearts and lives of others.

In addition to this, chapter four focussed on Paul as a godly example to his Corinthian converts (1 Cor 10:31–11:1; cf. 9:19-23). His goal of *saving many* was an essential element in the pattern he set before them and should be their objective as well as his own. Paul expected them to be committed to evangelism as he was (even if along different lines) and his ambitions were to be theirs.

The question now arises as to whether there is any concrete evidence in Paul's epistles which points to an active outreach on the part of believers for the spread of the gospel, or exhortations of the apostle urging them to engage in such activity. In our judgment there are two pertinent areas which should be investigated: the first has to do with the progress or advance of the gospel in Philippians, while the second concerns the spiritual warfare of Ephesians 6.

We shall turn to these important questions before commenting on Bowers' significant presentation.

---

11   W. P. Bowers, 'Church and Mission', 107.

The Advance of the Gospel

We have shown elsewhere that Paul often goes out of his way to stress the dynamic, almost personal, character of the gospel (εὐαγγέλιον/*euangelion*).[12] It is well-known that gospel within the Pauline corpus signifies not only the content of what is preached, but also the act or process of the proclamation (εὐαγγέλιον/*euangelion* is a noun of agency). The two are closely related and in the very act of proclamation the gospel's content becomes a reality. But, in addition, Paul speaks of the gospel as a force or agency able to accomplish something, and which has a purpose towards which it moves.[13] So in Colossians 1 εὐαγγέλιον/*euangelion* is a mighty, personal force working powerfully in the lives of men and women. It had come to the Colossian Christians (v. 6) and remained with them, having a firm place in their lives. Like the seed in the parable of the sower it continued to produce a vigorous fruit (Luke 8:15), not only among the Colossians themselves (Col 1:10) but also in the rest of the world. 'Fruit-bearing' is to be understood as a crop of good deeds (cf. Phil 1:11), while the growth of the gospel points to the increasing number of converts.

The dynamic character of the gospel is accented in 1 Thessalonians 1 (Paul's first introductory thanksgiving paragraph). At v. 5 though he might well have written 'we came with the gospel' (cf. 2 Cor 10:14), here by stating 'our gospel came', he puts the emphasis on the activity of the message. The manner of its coming was truly awesome, for it was not simply in word but also 'in power and in the Holy Spirit and with full conviction'. Gospel is again regarded as a personal, living force (cf. 2 Thess 3:1). Furthermore, its dynamic activity did not cease with the expulsion of the missionaries from Thessalonica. Paul's reference at 2:13 brings out this point: the 'word of God' (here synonymous with εὐαγγέλιον/*euangelion*), which the Thessalonian believers welcomed into their hearts, is said to be continually effective in their midst. Not only was the gospel active when they first

---

12 P. T. O'Brien, 'Thanksgiving and the Gospel in Paul', *NTS* 21 (1974-75), 144-155, and 'The Importance of the Gospel', 213-233.

13 In our treatment of 1 Corinthians 9:23 we have understood εὐαγγέλιον/*euangelion* in this dynamic sense and argued that Paul is referring to his own participation in the gospel's powerful advance.

believed; even now their continued Christian existence was dependent on it.

Under this heading of the advance of the gospel we propose to look at two examples: the first has to do with unnamed believers, probably in Rome, who declared the word of God boldly, while the second concerns the Philippians and their commitment to the gospel.

(a) Speaking the Word of God boldly (Phil 1:14)

Philippians 1:14–18 bears incidental, but important, testimony to the work of evangelism by Christian men and women in the city of Paul's imprisonment which was probably Rome. The apostle writes confidently to his dear friends at Philippi, who had been deeply concerned about his welfare, to assure them that the things that had happened to him, namely, his imprisonment, sufferings and personal inconveniences, had surprisingly contributed to the *progress* (προκοπή/*prokopē*) of the gospel. That dynamic advance, which was of paramount importance to Paul, since he read his own circumstances in the light of it, is described in two ways: first, outside the Christian community his arrest and confinement were understood to be because of his union with Christ. He was not in prison as a political or civil wrong-doer; instead, his detention was a demonstration or manifestation of Christ's saving activity and thus contributed to the spread of the gospel among those who made up the praetorian guard, as well as among other Gentiles (v. 13). Secondly, others within the Christian fellowship had been given fresh stimulus for the work of evangelism (v. 14). The majority of believers in the city had already been proclaiming Christ before Paul arrived there. But now with his imprisonment their confidence in the Lord had been strengthened by his example and they had been encouraged to testify to Christ more courageously. Clearly, the preaching of the gospel is a highly significant motif in this paragraph, and Paul knows of its progress in the capital because of what he had observed.

Even when Christians preached Christ from improper motives (vv. 15, 17–18), the apostle could still rejoice that his Lord was 'proclaimed', and that the apostolic kerygma was making dynamic headway. Clearly, for Paul, the courageous speaking out by believers of the word of God, even if some were moved by 'jealousy and rivalry' (v. 15), was ground for exulting in God.

To sum up. Several important points emerge from this passage: first, the apostle's reference to Christians in Rome engaging in evangelism appears to be an incidental one, but is all the more significant for that reason. As Paul writes to his Philippian friends he expresses no surprise that these believers should engage in active outreach for the gospel. Secondly, these Christians were already evangelizing prior to his arrival in the city. Now, through Paul's witness in prison, they are galvanized into speaking the word of God with 'greater boldness and without fear'. Thirdly, Paul obviously approved of this energetic activity. He rejoices when their resolve to evangelize is strengthened (whether from the highest motives or not), and he regards their proclamation of Christ as a significant element in the advance of the gospel. Finally, it appears to have been individual Christians, rather than a church as church, who were engaged in this praiseworthy endeavour.

(b) The Philippians' commitment to the gospel (Phil 1:5, 27, 30; 2:16)

If this first reference to believers evangelizing in Rome appears to be an incidental one (Phil 1:14–18), then the second group of texts is not. Paul refers several times, either by way of commendation or exhortation, to the Philippians' commitment to the gospel. How much these passages are actually saying is disputed. Paul Bowers, for example, claims that Paul did not envisage his churches as being independent instruments of active mission. Even where a positive outreach by believers appears to be in view, it is not a deliberate mission on the Pauline model. Rather, congregations 'render support to a particular mission, a support which emerges in the circumstances not as a general function of the life of these churches *qua* churches, but as a function of their relationship with Paul, the one who under God fathered their communities and therefore merits their continuing fellowship'.[14] They are encouraged to support his mission by prayer and financial support, thus becoming partners with him in it.

But is this all that the apostle is saying when he speaks of the Philippians' partnership in this dynamic gospel? Given that the

---

14   W. P. Bowers, *Studies*, 118; cf. 'Church and Mission', 101–102.

term ἐκκλησία/*ekklēsia* has particular reference to the congregation as gathered, it is not the Philippian church *as church* which is engaged in evangelism or an independent instrument of active mission. But this is not to rule out the possibility of individual believers, alone or collectively, proclaiming the gospel to non-Christians. In order to determine whether this is so, we survey the relevant texts.[15]

1. Partnership in the gospel (1:5)

This key expression turns up in Paul's introductory thanksgiving paragraph and provides the second basis of his thanks to God: '[I am grateful] for your active participation (κοινωνία/*koinōnia*) in the gospel from the first day until now'. Although the term κοινωνία/*koinōnia* has been taken in a passive sense, so that the whole phrase, 'your participation in the gospel', is regarded as equivalent to 'your faith' and means that they had received the gospel, it is better to understand the word in an active sense signifying 'your co-operation [in promoting] the gospel'.

Paul has in mind a dynamic endeavour on the part of the Philippians. Their active partnership was with him in his ministry of the word of life to Gentiles and is to be understood in a broad sense. Their co-operation is not limited to their financial help, though clearly this was in the apostle's mind, since it was referred to in v. 3 (cf. 4:15-18), and was a signal instance of their κοινωνία/*koinōnia*.

Their 'participation', as I shall endeavour to show, also included their actual proclamation of the gospel message to outsiders (see below on 1:27, 30) and their suffering along with Paul for the gospel's sake (cf. 1:30; 4:14-15). Furthermore, it involved their intercessory activity on his behalf (cf. 1:19), an endeavour in which the apostle knew they were engaged at the time of his writing to them.

2. Contending for the faith of the gospel (1:27, 30)

Paul submitted his own personal interests to the wider concerns of the gospel. He also desired that the Philippians, whose circumstances were different from his own and who were not missionaries as he was, might measure their lives by the yardstick of

---

15   For a more detailed examination see my article, 'The Importance of the Gospel', 216-226, and at the relevant exegetical points of my commentary, *Philippians*.

this powerful message. So he admonishes them with what is the central exhortation of the letter: 'Now the important thing is this: as citizens of heaven live in a manner that is worthy of the gospel of Christ' (v. 27). This exhortation is both crucial and comprehensive for it covers every aspect of their lives. It would involve the Philippians standing fast or secure (στήκετε/*stēkete*) with a common purpose ('in one spirit') in the face of attacks upon the gospel's progress. The following clauses explain positively (v. 27b, 'struggling for the faith of the gospel') and negatively (v. 28, 'in no way letting your opponents intimidate you') what this remaining steadfast signifies.

The verb συναθλέω/*synathleō* originally an athletic metaphor meaning to 'contend, struggle along with', draws attention to the point that the Philippians are to present a united front against the attacks of the enemy in their conflict for the gospel. Although the notions of hostility and persecution are present in the context, V. C. Pfitzner draws attention to the positive aspects of the struggle: its 'purpose . . . is not the conquest and defeat of the enemy as such, but the spread and growth of [the] faith, the same goal which was set before all Paul's work'.[16] Here the stress is on unity and the need for a concerted effort among the Philippians: they are to 'contend as one man' (note the prefix συν/*syn* of the verb συναθλέω/*synathleō* 'struggle with').

By standing firm in the face of attacks made upon the gospel, Paul's Christian friends show that their goal is the same as his own, namely, the spread and growth of the faith which arises from this εὐαγγέλιον/*euangelion*. Although their circumstances differ, Paul and the Philippians are engaged in the same struggle (ἀγών/*agōn*, v. 30), that is, a contest for the gospel and its progress.

We have noted elsewhere that Philippians 1:27-30 is a crucial passage which contains the *central* exhortation of the epistle.[17] Now for another reason this short paragraph is seen to be highly significant: it throws light on our inquiry into whether the Philippians' participation in the gospel involved them in evangelistic outreach or not. We have already observed that these friends were identified with the apostle in his missionary endeavours, a participation that included their financial support,

---

16   V. C. Pfitzner, *Paul and the Agon Motif* (Leiden: Brill, 1967), 116-117.

17   P. T. O'Brien, 'The Gospel and Godly Models', and *Philippians*, 143-162.

prayer and encouragement of the apostle. But the meaning of their partnership (κοινωνία/*koinōnia*) cannot be limited to their involvement in Paul's endeavours, for in 1:27-30 he encourages them to stand firm *at Philippi*, to present a united front against the attacks of the enemy in their own city, not in the place of Paul's captivity. The ἀγών/*agōn* ('struggle') in which they were engaged, as we have seen, was for the mighty advance of the gospel. The Philippians had the same goal as the apostle himself, and in this context it must include their speaking the word of the Lord boldly. This is not to suggest that their evangelistic outreach took the same form as Paul's. However, their commitment to the kerygma involved being caught up with its dynamic movement in Philippi, as well as being obligated to Paul in his missionary endeavours.

3. Holding fast the word of life (2:16)

In the light of the foregoing, the apostle's encouragement to the Philippians to 'hold fast the word of life' takes on added meaning. Paul clarifies how they can fulfil their responsibility of behaving as God's children in the world. He has already urged his friends at Philippi to 'do everything without grumbling and quarreling' because he wants them to be blameless and pure in the midst of an unbelieving world—a world that stands under divine judgment, although it is not entirely without hope (vv. 14-15). These Christians have replaced Israel as God's people and shine in the world like stars lighting up the sky, a privilege that had belonged to Israel of old. They already share Christ's risen life and anticipate the ministry of the resurrection age.

In the expression 'holding fast the word of life' the verb ἐπέχω/*epechō* could be translated 'holding *forth* [that word]'. If this rendering is correct, then Paul is referring to the missionary and evangelistic influence of the Philippian Christians who offer the word of life to others for acceptance. However, on contextual and linguistic grounds 'hold[ing] fast' is preferable. This meaning is well attested outside the NT,[18] and the general context of Philippians 1:27-2:18 has to do with standing firm in the faith against the attacks of external opponents. As these believers 'hold fast the word of life' they will prevent disunity from extinguishing the testimony; and if the apostolic testimony is held firm, then Paul

---

18   See BAGD, 285.

will have no cause for shame or regret that his work at Philippi had failed (v. 16b).

However, *holding fast* the word (λόγος/*logos*) of life is not to be interpreted in a passive or restricted sense. Paul's expression does not suggest keeping the message to oneself, enfolding it in one's bosom, as it were. This λόγος/*logos* is both a proclamation of the true life that is found in Christ and the word that creates life. It is synonymous with the gospel which is explosive and cannot be contained. It is open-ended. As the Philippians hold fast to it, against opposition from outsiders, this powerful message is able to demolish the strongholds of human arguments and overthrow the lofty imaginations of men and women, taking every thought captive to obey Christ (2 Cor 10:4-5). And as the message makes its triumphal march throughout the world, the Philippians, like Paul, are carried along by it as they bear testimony to the lordship of Jesus Christ.

To conclude. Under our heading of the advance of the gospel the two examples from Paul's Letter to the Philippians have led to the following conclusions: first, the apostle expresses no surprise that in the place of his imprisonment believers were engaged in active evangelism and had been doing so prior to his arrival there. His own firm stand for Christ while in prison had galvanized them into further courageous action. Secondly, the Philippians' fellowship in the gospel meant that they were committed to Paul's mission, through prayer, financial support and by other means. But their κοινωνία/*koinōnia* was not limited to their involvement in Paul's endeavours: they were engaged in the same struggle for the gospel as he was (1:30), albeit *in Philippi*, and thus their contending for the spread and growth of the faith signified evangelistic outreach. Likewise, their holding fast the word of life, which Paul encourages them in (2:16), included among other things their letting this explosive message have its dynamic way in and through their lives as it made its triumphal progress in Philippi.

The Spiritual Warfare of Ephesians 6

[10] Finally, be strong in the Lord and in his mighty power. [11] Put on the full armor of God so that you can take your stand against the devil's schemes. [12] For our struggle is not against flesh and blood, but against the rulers, against the

authorities, against the powers of this dark world and against the spiritual forces of evil in the heavenly realms. [13] Therefore put on the full armor of God, so that when the day of evil comes, you may be able to stand your ground, and after you have done everything, to stand. [14] Stand firm then, with the belt of truth buckled around your waist, with the breastplate of righteousness in place, [15] and with your feet fitted with the readiness that comes from the gospel of peace. [16] In addition to all this, take up the shield of faith, with which you can extinguish all the flaming arrows of the evil one. [17] Take the helmet of salvation and the sword of the Spirit, which is the word of God. [18] And pray in the Spirit on all occasions with all kinds of prayers and requests. With this in mind, be alert and always keep on praying for all the saints. [19] Pray also for me, that whenever I open my mouth, words may be given me so that I will fearlessly make known the mystery of the gospel, [20] for which I am an ambassador in chains. Pray that I may declare it fearlessly, as I should.

Our concerns in this chapter have been twofold: first, to examine the evidence in one of Paul's epistles, at least, which points to an active outreach on the part of believers for the spread of the gospel, and, secondly, to investigate exhortations of the apostle which urge them to engage in evangelism.

As we turn to the second of these concerns, it is surprising to observe how little attention has been paid to Paul's statements about the spiritual warfare in Ephesians 6:10-20, especially the reference to believers having their feet shod with 'the preparation of the gospel of peace' (v. 15) and their being urged to use the sword of the Spirit, namely, the word of God, as an offensive weapon (v. 17). These two verses have particular significance for our investigation.

(a) Spiritual warfare and the issue of power

As we examine vv. 15 and 17 we note that they are part of a unique emphasis on spiritual warfare and power found in Ephesians 6:10-20 where believers are called upon to struggle against evil and personal, supernatural forces called 'principalities and powers'.[19] This paragraph is neither an appendix to the letter nor a parenthesis

---

19   Note particularly the recent ground-breaking works of C. E. Arnold, *Ephesians: Power and Magic* (Cambridge: University Press, 1989), 103-122, and *Powers of Darkness* (Leicester: Inter-Varisty, 1992), 148-160, to which I am especially indebted.

within it. Instead, the passage has an important structural role in Ephesians, although surprisingly few writers have adequately explained its function. It brings the theme of power to a climax by focussing on the power of God working on behalf of believers in their struggle with the forces of evil.

Paul's Letter to the Ephesians stresses in a most emphatic way the saving and enabling power of God. The apostle's prayer of chapter 1 together with its counterpart and doxology in the third chapter show clearly that God's power is a key motif in the epistle.[20] His might brings about salvation and enables believers to love in the way that Christ did. This power is imparted through our union with Christ and because of his indwelling our lives. The stress on God's power in the first half of the letter provides the basis and sets the stage for the exhortatory material that follows in chapters 4 to 6.

At the same time the epistle has more to say about evil powers and the right Christian response to them than any other NT letter.[21] The range of terms used as well as the space given over to the subject makes this point plain. Paul does not demythologize the powers by making them equivalent to abstract notions like 'flesh' and 'sin', or by regarding them as some kind of spiritual atmosphere; instead, he reflects 'the prevailing Jewish and Hellenistic view of a belief in the reality of evil spirit-beings'.[22] The apostle's pastoral and theological intention is to explain Christ's lordship over the principalities and where the readers, in the light of their past and present union with Christ in his death and resurrection, stand in relation to the powers.

The teaching of chapters 1-3 on the 'powers' also anticipates the important paraenesis of 6:10-20. There are close verbal and structural links between the two prayers and doxology (chaps. 1, 3) and our paragraph that speaks of the conflict with the powers. Paul is addressing a group of believers, probably in western Asia Minor (through his circular letter), on the nature of the Christian life in the light of the ongoing hostility of evil, supernatural powers.[23]

The apostle depicts the Christian life *as a whole* being a spiritual struggle. Every believer is involved in it for his words in 6:10-20

---

20 Note C. E. Arnold, *Ephesians*, 70-102, esp. 102.

21 Note C. E. Arnold, *Ephesians*, 41-69, esp. 69.

22 C. E. Arnold, *Ephesians*, 69.

23 C. E. Arnold, *Ephesians*, 102.

are addressed to each and every reader. In the preceding paragraph, the household table of Ephesians 5:21–6:9, he had some important things to say to *different members* of Christian households, namely, to wives and husbands, children and parents, slaves and masters. But now he addresses *everyone* in the congregations (Ephesians may well be a circular letter) with his vital words about the spiritual struggle and the armour of God. In this radical description Christians are represented as facing intense attacks from the devil and his hosts.

According to Ephesians 2:1-3 men and women outside of Christ are 'dead in their trespasses and sins'. They are deeply affected by evil, determining influences: described in terms of the environment ('the age of this world'), an inner inclination towards evil ('the flesh') and a supernaturally powerful opponent ('the prince of the power of the air, the spirit that is now at work among those who are disobedient').[24] Separation from God's presence is inescapable for non-Christians unless they experience God's perfect gift of forgiveness and new life.

But this is not all. These evil influences continue to make themselves felt even after someone is united to Christ. A believer is not automatically immune to temptation or the attacks of Satan and his hosts. In a context of godly behaviour Christians are urged 'not to make room for the devil' (Eph 4:27). There is of course a decisive difference for the child of God. He or she lives in union with the risen Christ and may draw on his almighty power— available through his victory on the cross—to resist the world's influences and the fiery darts of the evil one. The warfare continues, however, for although Christ's victory over the powers of darkness is a significant one, that victory remains hidden. Satan and his hosts continue to exist in order to make war on the saints, even though their time is short and their ultimate overthrow fixed by God (Rev 20:3).

Paul employs a vivid expression to depict this spiritual warfare. It is a word rendered 'struggle' (πάλη/*palē*) which is found nowhere else in the Greek Bible. This term was common in the first century, not in a context of warfare, but in the sport of wrestling. The blue ribbon event in the ancient games of Ephesus and other cities of Asia Minor was not the marathon or the hundred metre dash, but the 'struggle' in wrestling. The apostle

---

24   C. E. Arnold, *Powers of Darkness*, 152.

states that, in contrast to this 'flesh and blood' wrestling with which the Ephesians would have been familiar, the true struggle of believers is a spiritual power encounter that requires spiritual weaponry. Paul may have used this term drawn from wrestling in order to emphasize the closeness of the battle with the powers of evil. It is hand to hand combat that is in view, not the firing of computer guided missiles from a distance!

As Christians engage in this momentous struggle they need to be clear about their *chief goal*. Put simply, it is to 'stand'. Four times in the passage Paul uses words from the same Greek root meaning to *stand/withstand* (vv. 11, 13 [twice], 14). The chief exhortation of the passage is the imperative of v. 14 στῆτε/*stēte* ('stand').[25] Arnold comments that the whole of vv. 14-20 is dependent on this main idea of v. 14. 'All other thoughts are subservient to this ultimate aim'.[26] The strength which God promises to supply, then, is for the purpose that we might be able to stand against the principalities and successfully resist them. The exhortation to acquire divine strength by putting on the armour of God is not an end in itself. It is provided for the fulfilment of this goal of standing firm.

(b) Spiritual warfare as resistance

As the believer engages in this conflict, one aspect that the apostle has particularly in view is *resistance* to temptation. In the wider context of Ephesians it is clear that he does not want Christians to 'give place to the devil', particularly by succumbing to any moral impurity (Eph 4:27; cf. 2:2-3). Resisting temptation is a *defensive posture* which is absolutely crucial. It involves recognizing the supernatural power of temptation and being prepared to face it. This can only be done through God's almighty power, hence it is essential to 'be strong in the Lord and in his great might' (v. 10). To do this is to put on 'the whole armour of God' (v. 11). The full range of equipment is to be used against enemy aggression so as to maintain the ground which belongs to those in Christ.

---

25 J. Gnilka, *Der Epheserbrief* (Freiburg: Herder, 1980), 309, and R. Schnackenburg, *The Epistle to the Ephesians* (Edinburgh: Clark, 1991), 268-269.

26 C. E. Arnold, *Ephesians*, 106.

(c) Spiritual warfare as proclamation

The second response expected of believers as we 'stand firm' is one of proclamation. Paul's readers were not only to be on the defensive in their spiritual warfare by not giving ground to the powers of darkness; they were also to take the offensive against Satan and his hosts. In fact, the movement of the whole passage shows that Paul thinks of standing firm particularly in terms of being on the offensive. How this is done the apostle spells out in vv. 15 and 17 (cf. v 19).

(1) Put on shoes for spreading the gospel (v. 15)

Paul calls the soldiers of Christ to advance on enemy territory by fearlessly declaring the gospel of the Lord Jesus. Just as Jesus first bound the strong man in order to plunder his house and his goods, so too we are to plunder Satan's kingdom by proclaiming the gospel, the message of rescue, to men and women held captive in the kingdom of darkness.

As he exhorts his readers Paul mentions the all-round equipment which protects the fighter on all sides and makes him ready for the battle. The whole description is characterized by references and allusions to OT passages. It is God's own armour that is in view; he is the warrior who, so to speak, uses these weapons (cf. Isa 42:13; 59:17; Hab 3:8-9; Ps 35:1-3). Paul's account, then, in Ephesians 6 is intended to drive home the point that the believer is equipped by God with his own armour. At the same time, the apostle is less concerned with the weapons and articles of clothing themselves than the function that each has.[27]

The belt and shoes are not weapons in the real sense but are simply part of the warrior's clothing. For Roman soldiers the short boots (*caliga*) were a necessary part of their equipment. A typical soldier would journey for miles, as his army advanced to the battefront, and then pursue the enemy. The footwear the Christian needs to use is 'the readiness to announce the gospel of peace'. As believers we need to be prepared to share the gospel of Christ wherever God may lead us.

---

27   Cf. R. Schnackenburg, *Ephesians*, 276-277.

(2) Take the sword of the Spirit which is the word of God (v. 17)

The sole offensive weapon mentioned in this panoply of God is the sword. While it obviously helped the believer's resistance, it was also a weapon of aggression. The sword of the Spirit is identified with the word of God, and we should be in no doubt that this refers to the gospel (cf. Rom 10:8). At v. 15 Paul spoke of the 'readiness' of the Christian warrior to make known the gospel. Now he goes a step further and mentions the power by which that gospel is successful, namely, the Spirit. 'The Word of God and the work of the Spirit are the means by which the people of God step out in defiance of Satan and rob his domain'.[28] These are the instruments by which God draws men and women into a relationship with himself, transforming their lives so as to be like his Son.

All Christians are involved in this spiritual warfare against the powers of darkness. Each and every believer is to stand firm against the onslaughts of the evil one by resistance and by proclamation. The primary aggressive action the Christian is called upon to take is the spreading of the gospel in the world—the good news of salvation through the death and resurrection of Christ.

The whole course of Paul's ministry was 'a model of this aggressive proclamation'. Luke's accounts in the Book of Acts, to which we have made passing reference, emphasize this point of Paul's missionary outreach again and again. Christian men and women should follow this lead. Our circumstances may be vastly different from Paul's; our spiritual gifts and opportunities may vary significantly from his. But we are involved in the same spiritual warfare as the apostle, we have the same injunction laid upon us to stand firm, the same divine weapons available for us to use (especially the essential spiritual weapon of prayer), and the same defensive and offensive postures to adopt. We are to resist temptation and to devote our lives energetically to spreading the gospel. These are not optional extras. They are musts and this is why the apostle's words about sharing the gospel effectively in the power of the Spirit wherever we find ourselves may be styled 'The Pauline Great Commission'.

---

28 C. E. Arnold, *Powers of Darkness*, 157.

Concluding Summary

It is time to draw together the threads and summarize our conclusions. First, there is clear evidence in the Letter to the Philippians of an active outreach on the part of believers for the spread of the gospel. Some were engaged in evangelism in the capital prior to Paul's arrival there and, because of his own firm stand for Christ, their resolve to speak the word of God with greater boldness was strengthened. Further, in the same letter it is clear that the Philippians' partnership in the gospel meant they were not only engaged in the apostle's mission but were also committed to evangelistic outreach in their own city.

Secondly, according to Ephesians 6 all Christians are involved in a spiritual warfare in which they are to *stand firm* against the onslaughts of the evil one by resistance and proclamation. The believer is boldly to make known the gospel of salvation in and through the mighty power of the Holy Spirit.

Thus, instances of believers actually evangelizing, and exhortations to engage in this worthy enterprise (Eph 6; cf. Col 4:5-6) have been reviewed in two of the apostle's letters. In the light of this limited evidence we return to Bowers' important presentation in order to make some observations and evaluation:

1. Bowers claims that in Paul's letters there are very few references to an active outreach for the spread of the gospel and the founding of new believing communities. He allows, in relation to Colossians 4:5-6, that Christians are seen in an evangelistic role, although this is not on the pattern of Paul's own work. Instead, it is 'a ministry of attraction and responsiveness rather than one of deliberate outreach and active solicitation'.[29] He calls it 'a stationary rather than a mobile witness'.

But even if Bowers is right in contending that this witness is not strictly on the Pauline model, there are more examples of evangelism actually occurring than he is prepared to admit. The two instances mentioned in Philippians should be included in the count. Furthermore, against Bowers, Paul commends them for this witness. Philippians 1:14-18 refers positively to unnamed believers who were committed to the progress of the gospel, while the Christians at Philippi were commended by the apostle for their

---

29   W. P. Bowers, *Studies*, 116; cf. 'Church and Mission', 101.

efforts in this regard (cf. Phil 2:15-16 in the light of 1:5, 27-30). (The references in Romans 1:8 and 1 Thessalonians 1:8 are admittedly disputed.)[30] There may be fewer instances of evangelistic outreach in the Pauline letters than we would expect. But the reason for this (as we indicate below) lies in Paul's preference for speaking about the dynamic progress of the gospel.

2. It has already been shown that the establishment of settled congregations was an important goal of Paul's missionary strategy. This is not to suggest, however, that believers within these churches had no further responsibility to outsiders. The apostle urged his Philippian friends to 'hold fast' the word of life (2:15-16). This did not signify keeping the message to themselves, or enfolding it safely in their arms so that others could not receive it. The gospel was dynamic, even explosive, and could not be contained. It was making its triumphal progress throughout the world, including Philippi, and the Christian residents of that city were caught up in its onward march. Even Paul himself was carried along by this powerful message: at 1 Thessalonians 1:5, instead of telling his readers, 'we came with the gospel', he states, 'our gospel came'; it was like a person with an authority of its own leading the apostle along. One might compare the Lucan summaries in the Book of Acts where powerful, personal activities are ascribed to the word of the Lord: so at 19:20 it is said to have grown mightily and prevailed.

Bower's treatment, in my judgment, has not taken sufficient account of this dynamic progress of the gospel. Paul speaks of it in a variety of ways in his letters. When he refers to the fulfilment of the divine purposes, instead of focussing on what men and women are doing, he regularly highlights this powerful advance of the kerygma. An important reference in support of this is 2 Thessalonians 3:1-2, where the apostle requests his Christian friends as follows: 'brothers and sisters, pray for us'. The content of the petition is not that Paul and his colleagues may speak the word

---

30 After an exegetical analysis of 1 Thessalonians 1:8, Bowers, *Studies*, 112, claims that 'Paul is not reporting on the spread of the gospel from the Thessalonians out among the public but is rather continuing his theme that the events at Thessalonica have proved an inspiration to believers everywhere'. Even if there has been some measure of public gossip about events in Thessalonica, Paul is speaking of something happening to them, not something they are doing. The issue of an example remains as the focus of attention. Cf. Romans 1:8.

boldly and clearly, though he might well have requested this (cf. Eph 6:19; Col 4:3-4); rather, it is that 'the word of the Lord may *run* (lit. τρέχη/ *trechē*) and be glorified, just as it is among you'. Paul and others will be doing the preaching but the stress is on the dynamic march of the εὐαγγέλιον/ *euangelion* itself. (In fact, the apostle has gone out of his way to make this point emphatically, for in v. 2 he swings back to the first person plural subject, 'and that *we* may be rescued from wicked and evil people'.) Even in Philippians 1 the bold speaking of the word of God by believers in Rome is explained in terms of the gospel's progress (προκοπή/ *prokopē*). It is the divine work that the apostle consistently stresses and, although the evangelistic endeavours of Christians are mentioned from time to time, Paul regularly focusses on the ultimate source, namely, God's powerful saving action in the kerygma. In our view, this explains the relative paucity of references to Christians engaging in evangelism.

3. Against Bowers we have shown (in the fourth chapter) that in 1 Corinthians 10:33–11:1 explicitly, and elsewhere implicitly, the apostle's exhortation to imitation was an admonition to engage in evangelistic outreach. His goal of saving many was an essential element in the servant pattern he adopted ('I have made myself a slave to all, so that I might win as many as possible', 1 Cor 9:19), and should have been the Corinthians' objective as well as his own. Paul expected them to be committed to evangelism just as he was (though the precise form this might take could vary), and his ambitions were to be theirs.

Paul does distinguish himself from his converts, as Bowers argues, not least when he is speaking about *his role* for them in the divine economy. His own involvement in the Gentile mission is traced back to a personal summons. It is agreed that he does not account for his calling by describing it as something 'natural to Christian experience but by explaining it as something quite particular to his own experience'.[31] However, when he urges the Corinthians to adopt the same goal that he has, namely, of winning others, his ground for doing so was his freedom in Christ, which they also possess. While it was in his encounter with the risen Christ that Paul was called to be an apostle and compelled to preach the gospel, the basis for his flexible conduct in different

---

31   W. P. Bowers, *Studies*, 106-107.

social settings, with its goal of winning many, lay in his being a Christian, not in his apostleship as such.

4. His requests for intercessory prayer by members of the churches he founded and his willingness to accept financial aid from some of them at least are bound up with their relationship to him and their continuing fellowship in the gospel. However, our study of Philippians 1:5, in the light of its immediate context and other significant statements in the letter (1:27, 30; 2:15-16), has shown that the addressees' κοινωνία/*koinōnia* in this gospel was not limited to this participation in Paul's ministry, significant though this was. The Philippians' struggle for the gospel signified evangelistic outreach as well, notably in their own city.

5. Bowers argues that even where there are references to an active outreach for the spread of the gospel, this is undertaken not by churches *as* churches, but 'through individual believers, alone or collectively, [who are] directed by God and assisted by church communities'.[32] He rejects the view that Paul's doctrine of the church, especially where it appeared to be experiencing a numerical increase that was being encouraged by its members, was clear evidence that the apostle regarded his churches as instruments of active, ongoing mission. Bowers in particular referred to the imagery of the church as a *building* in the process of construction (Eph 3:19-22) and of a *body* where growth is in view (Col 2:19; cf. Eph 4:16). He argued that the growth was either done to the church, not by it, or that it referred to a growth in maturity: 'Evangelistic activity by the church itself leading to such growth is not suggested'.[33]

The issue is a complex one which I have examined elsewhere.[34] It was concluded that when the apostle speaks of God's people as a church (ἐκκλησία/*ekklēsia*), temple, bride, body or the like, the focus of attention is upon relationships with God, Christ or between members. These images or pictures do not treat believers' relationships with the world. This is not to suggest that Christians have no responsibilities or duties to those outside of Christ. They

---

32   W. P. Bowers, 'Church and Mission', 107.

33   W. P. Bowers, *Studies*, 110. Cf. 110-112, and his recent article, 'Church and Mission', 95-97.

34   P. T. O'Brien, 'The Church as a Heavenly and Eschatological Entity', in *The Church in the Bible and the World*, ed. D. A. Carson (Exeter: Paternoster, 1987), 88-119, 307-311.

are, however, expressed by other terms and ideas, e.g. witnesses, debtors, those who proclaim God's mighty acts, etc.

Strictly speaking, then, Bowers is correct when he argues that an active outreach for the gospel is not undertaken by churches *as* churches, or the body as body.[35] Paul's use of ἐκκλησία/*ekklēsia* has to do with a gathering of God's people for worship, fellowship and edification, while the body image looks upwards and inwards but not outwards. However, the statement is misleading if it suggests that individual believers, either alone or assisted by other Christians in fellowship with them, are not to engage in evangelistic outreach. And, sad to say, this is what statements about the church having no mission are often taken to mean. The linguistic qualification is misunderstood and the arguments turn, in large measure, on semantic issues.

6. Bowers suggests that Paul does not seem to have enjoined on his readers an energetic, mobile missionary initiative of the sort he undertook. This was due, he claims, to the distinctive nature of Paul's calling as an apostle to the Gentiles. But while it is true that the calling and gifts of Paul's converts were different from his own, the logic of the gospel demanded that they be committed to its ongoing dynamic advance, whatever form it took. This commitment may not have resulted in mobile missionary initiatives. On the other hand, in some cases it might have done so. We just do not know. Bowers' is an argument from silence. (We might note the mobile missionary efforts of the disciples from Cyprus and Cyrene who proclaimed the Lord Jesus to the Hellenists [Greeks] in Antioch: Acts 11:19-20. Was this a missionary initiative of the sort Paul undertook?) Furthermore, the Pauline 'Great Commission' of Ephesians 6 shows that all believers in the apostle's churches were involved in a spiritual warfare in which they were to stand firm against the onslaughts of the evil one by resistance and *proclamation*. Every Christian was (and is) boldly to make known the message of salvation in and through the mighty power of the Holy Spirit, whatever form it takes, mobile or stationary.

7. Paul's own mission was intimately related to the saving purposes of God in which the gospel of the Lord Jesus Christ was

---

35   Though it might be claimed that an evangelist, as a member of the body of Christ, has a ministry to outsiders. Bowers (*Studies*, 112) concludes: 'It appears then that in the Pauline imagery of the church there is no clearly expressed notion of that church as an active instrument of mission'.

central. For a variety of reasons, as we have seen, believers are committed to and involved in that same gospel and in doing this they identify with God's gracious plan of salvation. They are caught up in the gospel's dynamic advance, even though they do not have the same key role that Paul, the missionary apostle, had in relation to Gentiles and the mystery. But they were (and we are) at one with the apostle by being involved in the same ἀγών/*agōn* ('struggle') for the gospel. At this point of the theology of the gospel, Paul's understanding of *his* mission and that of mission generally intersect.

The implications of these conclusions for us as Christians are obvious. Like St Paul we ought to be consumed by passion for the gospel of the Lord Jesus. It is wrong to assume that, because the apostle mentions Christians engaging in evangelism on only a few occasions, he had no great interest in the matter. He genuinely desired that believers should bear faithful witness to Jesus as Lord in the presence of their non-Christian friends. He was encouraged when the resolve of the Christians in Rome to speak the word of God with greater boldness was strengthened, and he thanked God for the Philippians' partnership in the gospel, a partnership that indicated they were committed to both his mission and evangelistic outreach in their own city. We are always in need of being stirred up to witness faithfully to Jesus as Lord before our non-Christian friends. It is rarely easy to do it, and it can often lead to opposition, as in the case of the Philippians.

All Christians are involved in a spiritual warfare against the powers of darkness. We are to put on the whole armour of God with the aim of *standing firm* against the onslaughts of the evil one by resistance and proclamation. Like those first century Christians we are boldly to make known the gospel of salvation in and through the mighty power of the Holy Spirit. The dynamic of the gospel demands that we be committed to its ongoing advance, whatever form it takes. This may result in mobile missionary initiatives; on the other hand, it may not. The precise form the spoken witness takes is really secondary; it does not need to follow the Pauline model exactly, since God will use us to bear witness to his Son in accordance with the gifts he has given us and in whatever contexts we are placed.

CHAPTER 6

CONCLUDING REMARKS

Our inquiry into Paul's teaching and example as a missionary had limited aims. We set out to discover what was distinctive about his calling and commissioning, and to determine what were the essential features of his ministry, including its goals and content, its motivating power and its results. Furthermore, because Paul was an apostle, a special kind of missionary, we sought to find out what we could about the place of his missionary calling and ministry within God's saving purposes.

Paul clearly expected his readers to emulate him in his goals, attitudes and behaviour. But was he in any sense a missionary paradigm and, if so, what are the characteristics of his model? For instance, was he an example to his converts in his commitment to gospel outreach?

As to the method adopted, my analysis was limited to a study of Paul's letters. Luke's accounts of his colleague's missionary activities in the Book of Acts, while important for a comprehensive treatment of Paul as a missionary, were used only in a supplementary way. Further, it was not possible to make a comprehensive inquiry of all the relevant material in the apostle's letters. Instead, each chapter of this book focussed on one major Pauline passage (with other supporting material) in order to throw light on the fundamental questions raised.

The first two chapters addressed the question of the distinctives in Paul's career as a missionary. In chapter 1 I looked at two important passages (Gal 1:11-17; Eph 3:1-13) which deal with the significance of his encounter with the risen Christ on the Damascus road. That encounter set the course for the remainder of his life and his calling to be an apostle to the Gentiles formed the basis of his theology. The gospel which came to Paul was a personal disclosure of Jesus Christ in which he saw God's Son as the risen and exalted one in his glory. This was the same message he was commissioned to proclaim among the Gentiles so that they too might be converted and brought into a living relationship with the Lord Jesus. From a salvation historical perspective this gospel which he preached is identified with the promise made to Abraham (Gal 3:8). As Paul proclaimed the kerygma and Gentiles were brought into a covenant relationship with the living God through faith, so the promises made to Abraham were in the process of being fulfilled.

God had set Paul apart for his service before he was born. Like Jeremiah he had stood in 'the council of the Lord' and his message was God's true word to the Gentiles. At the same time, the apostle's allusions to Isaiah suggest he was chosen by God to continue the work of the Lord's Servant.

As the apostle to the Gentiles Paul had a unique relationship to the mystery, God's open secret (Eph 3). This had to do with the divine purposes of salvation in which both Jews and Gentiles would be incorporated into the body of Christ. As a steward of this mystery Paul had the privilege of unfolding its wonder. So his missionary commission included both the preaching of the unsearchable riches of Christ to the Gentiles (v. 8) and, as an integral feature of that proclamation, the bringing to light for all to see how this hidden purpose of God was being put into effect (v. 9).

In chapter 2, which examined Romans 15:14-33, we saw that Paul provided a brief overview of his missionary career from its beginnings and described its amazing effects. He spelled out a number of its distinguishing marks: first, the whole of his apostolic ministry was totally dependent upon divine grace. The content of the missionary activity to which God had called him was 'the priestly duty of proclaiming the gospel of God'. Paul had acted on Christ's behalf by discharging his priestly responsibilities in relation to the cult itself, namely, the gospel of God, while the purpose of his commissioning, indeed his whole missionary career, was so 'that the offering of the Gentiles might be acceptable to God, sanctified by the Holy Spirit' (Rom 15:16). This same goal may be described in terms of Christ's lordship over the new people of God, namely, '*for* the obedience of the Gentiles' (v. 18), which refers not simply to their acceptance of the gospel, but also to their growth in Christian maturity and perfection. Thus, as God's special envoy to the nations Paul's missionary calling played a significant role within divine redemptive history.

The results of Paul's work were extraordinary. Christ, by his Spirit, had worked so effectively through his servant that from Jerusalem all the way round to Illyricum he had 'fulfilled the gospel of Christ' (Rom 15:19), an expression which means that he had engaged in primary evangelism, nurtured Christians and established settled congregations in key centres of the eastern Mediterranean. Paul made it his aim to preach Christ in pioneer situations, going to Gentiles who had never heard the gospel. He knew from the OT Scriptures that he was continuing the Servant of the Lord's ministry. He was consumed by passion for the lost, for these needy Gentiles who did not know that the Servant's vicarious work of redemption was for them. Paul's deep-seated concern was at one with the Lord's kindness who had sent his Servant to men and women in great need. And as Paul pursued his ambition of preaching Christ where he was not known, he found that this prophetic word of God from the OT was reliable, for people from many nations in the eastern Mediterranean began to *see* and *understand* that the Servant's saving work was for them.

In the following three chapters I attempted to address the question as to what Paul as a missionary had in common with other Christians. This was occasioned by the surprising fact that although the apostle makes a number of important statements in his letters about his own missionary calling and its place within God's purposes, he does not seem, at first glance, to say a great deal about how the Christians in his congregations were to carry on his work or to be caught up with his mission and so be involved in these saving purposes of God.

I concluded from Romans 1:1-17 that the gospel of the Lord Jesus Christ within the purposes of God provides the connecting link between Paul's own missionary activity and that of other believers. His total involvement in the gospel runs like a scarlet thread throughout the letter, from the first verse to the concluding doxology. Paul was wholly committed to this divine kerygma, *not simply* because of his own conversion and calling by God to minister to Gentiles, *but also* because of its essential place in salvation history. His own involvement in the gospel led to the ingathering of Gentiles into the covenant people of God. But the ingathering of the nations was vaster and greater than Paul's own contribution, however vital this was. Likewise the advance of the gospel in which he was significantly involved was occurring throughout the world, in the places where Paul was actively engaged *and* where others were hard at work evangelizing.

The dynamic of the gospel's logic meant for believers in Rome and for other Christians a deeper commitment to its ongoing, powerful advance, as well as to the person at its centre, Jesus Christ, God's Son. The implications for us are the same. We who have come under Jesus' rule as Lord must be wholly committed to the furtherance of those saving purposes in which Gentiles, along with Jews, are brought into obedience to him. If we have truly experienced the saving power of the gospel in our own lives and have the assurance of deliverance from the wrath to come on the final day, then we cannot be anything other than debtors to those for whom Christ died—just as Paul was a debtor to them. If we know the desperate plight of men and women under divine judgment—we ourselves had once been in this predicament—and that the gospel is the only hope for deliverance from the wrath to come, then we should be wholly involved in bringing it into the lives of others. This is not to suggest that other Christians have the same calling to ministry as Paul, that their gifts of evangelism are identical with his, or that they are to be itinerant and roving missionaries like the apostle to the Gentiles.

Paul presented himself on a number of occasions in his letters as a model to be followed by his readers. When he reminded his Christian friends of his pattern of behaviour he did so for practical and exhortatory purposes since he had an ethical dimension in view. To the Philippians his example served to underscore the central exhortation of the letter ('Now, the important thing is this: live as citizens of heaven in a manner that is worthy of the gospel of Christ', Phil 1:27), an injunction which is part of the leading proposition that they should stand firm in the gospel (1:27-30). However, given the close connection between the apostle's life-style and the gospel he proclaims (cf. Phil 1:12-26; 1 Thess 2:1-12), we questioned whether there was something more to Paul's being a pattern. Did it also involve a commitment to the spread of the gospel as well?

The key text that was examined in order to answer this question was 1 Corinthians 11:1, 'Follow my example, as I follow the example of Christ'. From a detailed study of this verse within the context of chapters 10 and 11, and especially in the light of Paul's 'defence' in chapter 9:19-23, I concluded that the apostle's earnest desire and goal of saving men and women was an essential element in the servant pattern he adopted ('I have made myself a slave to all, so that I might win as many as possible', 1 Cor 9:19). Paul was committed to the good of others and he defines this in terms of saving them (10:33).

When he describes the stance that characterized his whole missionary career (1 Cor 9:19-23), Paul makes the following points: first, the basis for his flexible conduct in a variety of (social) settings lay in his *freedom in Christ* and his total gospel orientation. His behaviour was grounded in his being a Christian, not in his apostleship as such. Also, his overall stance of making himself a slave (9:19) was paradigmatic for the Corinthians. As one who was truly free, he was living in conformity with the example of his Lord and thus showing a truly Christian life-style. He followed the servant model of his Master (cf. Phil 2:7); let the readers and other Christians do the same. As we have seen, the salvation of men and women was Paul's goal (1 Cor 9:19-23). His earnest desire was to win Jews, Gentiles and weak Christians, that is, to save them completely so that they would be pure and blameless at the second coming. The Corinthians' ambitions and ours too, should be the same. Finally, although his overall stance of making himself a slave (v. 19) was paradigmatic for the Corinthians, the actual outworking of this for his readers might vary. Paul is not suggesting that they should engage in the same wide-ranging, apostolic ministry in which he has been involved; but each *in his or her own way and according to their personal gifts* was to have the same orientation and ambitions as Paul himself, that is, of seeking by all possible means to save some. They were to be consumed by passion as he was!

The recurring and puzzling question that has arisen out of our study of Paul and the dynamic of the gospel has been: Why is so little written in the Pauline letters about the need for Christians to evangelize? Was it because believers in Paul's churches were consistently speaking about Jesus as Lord to their non-Christian friends, and therefore did not need to be urged to do so? This suggestion does not satisfactorily answer the question, for although believers in several of the Pauline congregations seem to have been active in evangelizing outsiders, we cannot be sure that this dynamic activity was occurring everywhere, unless it is being described in other, less obvious ways. There are indeed some examples of evangelism actually occurring: so Philippians 1:14-18 refers positively to unnamed believers committed to the progress of the gospel, while the Christians at Philippi were commended by the apostle for their efforts in this regard (cf. Phil 2:15-16 in the light of 1:5, 27-30). There are fewer references to evangelistic outreach in the Pauline letters than we would expect.

The answer to this riddle is to be sought in two directions:

First, when Paul refers to the fulfilment of the divine purposes, instead of focussing on what men and women are doing, he regularly highlights the *powerful advance of the gospel*. It is the divine work that the apostle frequently stresses and, although the evangelistic endeavours of Christians are mentioned from time to time, this is not where he usually puts the emphasis. An important reference in support of this is 2 Thessalonians 3:1-2, where the apostle requests his Christian friends as follows: 'brothers and sisters, pray for us'. The content of the petition is not that Paul and his colleagues may speak the word of the gospel boldly and clearly, though he might well have requested this (cf. Eph 6:19; Col 4:3-4); rather, it is that 'the word of the Lord may *run* and be glorified, just as it is among you'. Paul and others will be engaged in preaching but the stress is on the dynamic march of the gospel itself. (In fact, the apostle has gone out of his way to make this point emphatically, for in v. 2 he swings back to the first person plural subject, 'and that *we* may be rescued from wicked and evil people'.) Even in Philippians 1 the bold speaking of the word of God by believers in Rome is explained in terms of the gospel's progress. It is the divine work that the apostle consistently stresses and, in our view, this explains the relative paucity of references to Christians engaging in evangelism.

Secondly, what we have styled, perhaps incorrectly, the Pauline 'Great Commission' of Ephesians 6, shows that all believers in the apostle's churches were involved in a spiritual warfare in which they were to stand firm against the onslaughts of the evil one by resistance and *proclamation*. Every Christian was (and is) boldly to make known the message of salvation in and through the mighty power of the Holy Spirit, whatever form it takes, mobile or stationary.

Paul's own mission was intimately related to the saving purposes of God in which the gospel of the Lord Jesus Christ was central. For a variety of reasons, as we have seen, believers are committed to and involved in this same gospel; in this way we identify with God's gracious plan of salvation. We are caught up in the gospel's dynamic advance, even though we do not have the same key role that Paul, the missionary apostle, had in relation to Gentiles and the mystery. But we are at one with the apostle since we are involved in the same 'struggle' for the gospel (Phil 1:30). It is at this point regarding the gospel, that Paul's understanding of *his* mission and that of mission generally intersect.

We have already spelled out some of the implications of these conclusions for us as Christians. Like St Paul we ought to be consumed by passion for the gospel of the Lord Jesus. We are always in need of being stirred up to witness faithfully to Jesus as Lord before our non-Christian friends. It is rarely easy to do this, and it can often lead to opposition, as Christians in the Pauline churches discovered. Nevertheless, we should be committed to this glorious message of the grace of God.

We too are involved in a spiritual warfare against the powers of darkness. We are to put on the whole armour of God with the aim of *standing firm* against the onslaughts of the evil one by resistance and proclamation. Like those first century Christians we are boldly to make known the gospel of salvation in and through the mighty power of the Holy Spirit. The dynamic of the gospel demands that we be committed to its ongoing advance, whatever form it takes. This may result in mobile missionary initiatives; on the other hand, it may not. The precise form the spoken witness takes is really secondary; it does not need to follow the Pauline model exactly, since God will use us to bear testimony to his Son in accordance with the gifts he has given us and the opportunities he provides for us.

BIBLIOGRAPHY

Arnold, C. E.,   *Ephesians: Power and Magic* (Cambridge: University Press, 1989).

Arnold, C. E.,   *Powers of Darkness* (Leicester: Inter-Varsity, 1992).

Asting, R.,   *Die Verkündigung des Wortes im Urchristentum* (Stuttgart: Kohlhammer, 1939).

Barrett, C. K.,   *A Commentary on the First Epistle to the Corinthians* (London: Black, 1968).

Barrett, C. K.,   'I am not Ashamed of the Gospel', in *New Testament Essays* (London: SPCK, 1972), 116-143.

Barrett, C. K.,   'Paulus als Missionar und Theologe', *ZTK* 86 (1989), 18-32.

Barrett, C. K.,   'The Gentile Mission as an Eschatological Phenomenon', in *Eschatology and the New Testament. Essays in Honor of George Raymond Beasley-Murray*, ed. W. H. Gloer (Peabody, MA: Hendrickson, 1988), 65-75.

Barth, M.,   *Ephesians 1-3* (Garden City, NY: Doubleday, 1974).

Best, E.,   *Paul and his Converts* (Edinburgh: Clark, 1988).

Best, E.,   'The Revelation to Evangelize the Gentiles', *JTS* 35 (1984), 1-30.

Betz, H. D.,   *Galatians* (Philadelphia: Fortress, 1979).

Betz, O.,   'Die Vision des Paulus im Tempel. Apg. 22, 17-21, als Beitrag zur Deutung des Damaskuserlebnisses', *Verborum Veritas. Festschrift für G. Stählin*, ed. O. Böcher and K. Haacker (Wuppertal: Brockhaus, 1970), 113-123.

Blair, E. P.,   'Paul's Call to the Gentile Mission', *Biblical Research* 10 (1965), 19-33.

Bockmuehl, M. N. A.,   *Revelation and Mystery* (Tübingen: Mohr, 1990).

Bornkamm, G.,   *Paul* (London: Hodder, 1969).

Bornkamm, G.,   'The Missionary Stance of Paul in 1 Corinthians 9 and in Acts', in *Studies in Luke-Acts*, ed. L. E. Keck and J. L. Martyn (London: SPCK, 1968), 194-207.

Bosch, D.,   *Transforming Mission. Paradigm Shifts in Theology of Mission* (New York: Orbis, 1991).

Bowers, W. P.,   'Church and Mission in Paul', *JSNT* 44 (1991), 89-111.

Bowers, W. P.,   'Fulfilling the Gospel: The Scope of the Pauline Mission', *JETS* 30 (1987), 185-198.

Bowers, W. P.,   *Studies in Paul's Understanding of His Mission* (unpublished Ph. D. dissertation, Cambridge, 1976).

Brown, R. E.,   *The Semitic Background of the Term 'Mystery' in the New Testament* (Philadelphia: Fortress, 1968).

Bruce, F. F.,   *An Expanded Paraphrase of the Epistles of Paul* (Palm Springs, CA: Haynes, 1981).

Bruce, F. F.,   'Further Thoughts on Paul's Autobiography (Galatians 1:11–2:14)', in *Jesus und Paulus. Festschrift für W. G. Kümmel zum 70. Geburtstag*, ed. E. E. Ellis and E. Grässer (Göttingen: Vandenhoeck, ^{2}1978), 21-29.

Bruce, F. F.,   *The Epistle to the Galatians* (Grand Rapids: Eerdmans, 1982).

Bruce, F. F.,   *The Epistles to the Colossians, to Philemon, and to the Ephesians* (Grand Rapids: Eerdmans, 1984).

Bruce, F. F.,   *The Letter of Paul to the Romans* (London: Tyndale, 1963).

Campbell, W. S., *Paul's Gospel in an Intercultural Context. Jew and Gentile in the Letter to the Romans* (Frankfurt: Lang, 1991).

Caragounis, C. C.,*The Ephesian Mysterion. Meaning and Content* (Lund: Gleerup, 1977).

Carson, D. A.,   'Pauline Inconsistency: Reflections on 1 Corinthians 9.19-23 and Galatians 2.11-14', *Churchman* 100 (1986), 6-45.

Carson, D. A.,   'The Purpose of Signs and Wonders in the New Testament', in *Power Religion. The Selling Out of the Evangelical Church?* ed. M. S. Horton (Chicago: Moody, 1992), 89-118.

Conzelmann, H., *I Corinthians* (Philadelphia: Fortress, 1975).

Cranfield, C. E. B., *The Epistle to the Romans* 2 Vols. (Edinburgh: Clark, 1975, 1979).

Dabelstein, R.,   *Die Beurteilung der "Heiden" bei Paulus* (Frankfurt/Bern: Lang, 1981).

Dahl, N. A.,   'The Missionary Theology in the Epistle to the Romans', in *Studies in Paul. Theology for the Early Christian Mission* (Minneapolis: Augsburg, 1977), 70-94.

Daube, D.,   *The New Testament and Rabbinic Judaism* (London: Athlone, 1956).

De Boer, W. P., *The Imitation of Paul* (Kampen: Kok, 1962).

Dietzfelbinger, C., *Die Berufung des Paulus als Ursprung seiner Theologie* (Neukirchen-Vluyn: Neukirchener Verlag, 1985).

Driver, J.,   'Paul and Mission', in *Mission Focus. Current Issues,* ed. W. Schenk and A. F. Glasser (Scottdale, PA: Herald, 1980), 47-69.

Dunn, J. D. G.,   '"A Light to the Gentiles": the Significance of the Damascus Road Christophany for Paul', in *The Glory of Christ in the New Testament. Studies in Christology,* ed. L. D. Hurst and N. T. Wright (Oxford: Clarendon, 1987), 251-266.

Dunn, J. D. G.,   *Christology in the Making* (London: SCM, 1980).

Dunn, J. D. G.,   *Jesus and the Spirit* (London: SCM, 1975).

Dunn, J. D. G.,   *Romans 1-8, Romans 9-16* (Dallas: Word, 1988).

Dunn, J. D. G.,   'The Relationship between Paul and Jerusalem according to Galatians 1 and 2', *NTS* 28 (1982), 461-478.

Dupont, J.,   'The Conversion of Paul, and Its Influence on his Understanding of Salvation by Faith', in *Apostolic History and the Gospel. Biblical and Historical Essays Presented to F. F. Bruce,* ed. W. W. Gasque and R. P. Martin (Exeter: Paternoster, 1970), 176-194.

Ellison, H. L.,   'Paul and the Law—"All Things to All Men"', in *Apostolic History and the Gospel. Biblical and Historical Essays Presented to F. F. Bruce,* ed. W. W. Gasque and R. P. Martin (Exeter: Paternoster, 1970), 195-202.

Fee, G. D.,   *The First Epistle to the Corinthians* (Grand Rapids: Eerdmans, 1987).

Fee, G. D.,   'Εἰδωλόθυτα Once Again: An Interpretation of 1 Corinthians 8-10', *Bib* 61 (1980), 172-197.

Fitzmyer, J. A.,   'The Gospel in the Theology of Paul', in *To Advance the Gospel* (New York: Crossroad, 1981), 149-161.

Fung, R. Y. K., *The Epistle to the Galatians* (Grand Rapids: Eerdmans, 1988).

Garlington, D., 'The Obedience of Faith in the Letter to the Romans. Part I: The Meaning of ὑπακοὴ πίστεως (Rom 1:5; 16:26)', *WTJ* 52 (1990), 201-224.

Garlington, D., *'The Obedience of Faith'. A Pauline Phrase in Historical Context* (Tübingen: Mohr, 1991).

Gaventa, B. R., *From Darkness to Light. Aspects of Conversion in the New Testament* (Fortress: Philadelphia, 1986).

Gilliland, D. S., 'New Testament Contextualization: Continuity and Particularity in Paul's Theology', in *The Word Among Us. Contextualizing Theology for Mission Today*, ed. D. S. Gilliland (Dallas, TX: Word, 1983), 52-73.

Gnilka, J., *Der Epheserbrief* (Freiburg: Herder, 1980).

Green, M., *Evangelism in the early Church* (London: Hodder, 1970).

Gundry Volf, J. M., *Paul and Perseverance* (Tübingen: Mohr, 1990).

Haas, O., *Paulus der Missionar* (Münsterschwarzach: Vier Türme-Verlag, 1971).

Hahn, F., *Mission in the New Testament* (London: SCM, 1965).

Hansen, G. W., *Abraham in Galatians. Epistolary and Rhetorical Contexts* (Sheffield: Academic Press, 1989).

Harrisville, R. A., 'Paul: Justification and Mission', in *Bible and Mission*, ed. W. Stumme (Minneapolis, MI: Augsburg, 1986), 47-60.

Hengel, M., 'The Origins of the Christian Mission', in *Between Jesus and Paul. Studies in the Earliest History of Christianity* (London: SCM, 1983), 48-64.

Hengel, M., *The Son of God* (London: SCM, 1976).

Hultgren, A. J., *Paul's Gospel and Mission. The Outlook from his Letter to the Romans* (Philadelphia: Fortress, 1985).

Hurtado, L. W., *One God, One Lord* (Philadelphia: Fortress, 1988).

Jeremias, J., *Der Schlüssel zur Theologie des Apostels Paulus* (Stuttgart: Calwer, 1971).

Jewett, R., 'Paul, Phoebe, and the Spanish Mission', in *The Social World of Formative Christianity and Judaism. Essays in Tribute to H. C. Kee*, ed. J. Neusner, E. S. Frerichs, P. Borgen and R. Horsley (Philadelphia: Fortress, 1988), 142-161.

Judge, E. A., 'The Teacher as Moral Exemplar in Paul and in the Inscriptions of Ephesus', in *In the Fullness of Time: Biblical Studies in Honour of Archbishop Donald Robinson*, ed. D. Peterson and J. Pryor (Homebush West, NSW: Lancer, 1992), 185-201.

Käsemann, E., *Commentary on Romans* (Grand Rapids: Eerdmans, 1980).

Kasting, H., *Die Anfänge der urchristlichen Mission* (München: Kaiser, 1969).

Kettunen, M., *Der Abfassungszweck des Römerbriefes* (Helsinki: Suomalainen Tiedeakatemin, 1979).

Kim, S., *The Origin of Paul's Gospel* (Grand Rapids: Eerdmans, 1982).

Knox, J., 'Romans 15:14-33 and Paul's Conception of his Apostolic Mission', *JBL* 83 (1964), 1-11.

Legrand, L., *Unity and Plurality. Mission in the Bible* (Maryknoll, NY: Orbis, 1990).

Liechtenhan, R., *Die urchristliche Mission. Voraussetzungen, Motive und Methoden* (Zürich: Zwingli, 1946).

Lincoln, A. T., *Ephesians* (Dallas: Word, 1990).

Lindars, B., 'The Old Testament and Universalism in Paul', *BJRL* 69 (1987), 511-527.

Malherbe, A. J., *Paul and the Thessalonians* (Philadelphia: Fortress, 1987).

Martin, D. B., *Slavery as Salvation. The Metaphor of Slavery in Pauline Christianity* (New Haven: Yale University, 1990).

Merklein, H., *Das kirchliche Amt nach dem Epheserbrief* (München: Kösel, 1973).

Merklein, H., 'Zum Verständnis des paulinischen Begriffs "Evangelium"', in *Studien zu Jesus und Paulus* (Tübingen: Mohr, 1987), 279-295.

Meyer, B. F., *The Early Christians. Their World Mission and Self-Discovery* (Wilmington, DE: Glazier, 1986).

Meyer, H. A. W., *Critical and Exegetical Handbook to the Epistle to the Romans* 2 (Edinburgh: T. & T. Clark, [2]1876).

Miller, D. G., 'Pauline Motives for the Christian Mission', in *The Theology of the Christian Mission*, ed. G. H. Anderson (London: SCM, 1961), 72-84.

Minear, P., 'Gratitude and Mission in the Epistle to the Romans', in *The Obedience of Faith* (London: SCM, 1971), 102-110.

Mitton, C. L.,   *Ephesians* (London: Oliphants, 1976).

Molland, E.,   *Das paulinische Euangelion. Das Wort und die Sache* (Oslo: Dybwad, 1934).

Moo, D.,   *Romans 1-8* (Chicago: Moody, 1991).

Morris, L.,   *The Epistle to the Romans* (Leicester: Inter-Varsity; 1988).

Morris, L.,   'The Theme of Romans', in *Apostolic History and the Gospel. Biblical and Historical Essays Presented to F. F. Bruce*, ed. W. W. Gasque and R. P. Martin (Exeter: Paternoster, 1970), 249-263.

Munck, J.,   *Paul and the Salvation of Mankind* (London: SCM, 1959).

Nickle, K. F.,   *The Collection. A Study in the Strategy of Paul* (London: SCM, 1966).

O'Brien, P. T.,   *Colossians, Philemon* (Waco, TX: Word, 1982).

O'Brien, P. T.,   'Justification in Paul and Some Crucial Issues of the Last Two Decades', in *Right with God: Justification in the Bible and the World*, ed. D.A. Carson (Carlisle: Paternoster, 1992), 69-95, 263-268.

O'Brien, P. T.,   'Paul's Missionary Calling within the Purposes of God', in *In the Fullness of Time: Biblical Studies in Honour of Archbishop Donald Robinson*, ed. D. Peterson and J. Pryor (Homebush West, NSW: Lancer, 1992), 131-148.

O'Brien, P. T.,   'Thanksgiving and the Gospel in Paul', *NTS* 21 (1974-75), 144-155.

O'Brien, P. T.,   'The Church as a Heavenly and Eschatological Entity', in *The Church in the Bible and the World*, ed. D. A. Carson (Exeter: Paternoster, 1987), 88-119, 307-311.

O'Brien, P. T.,   *The Epistle to the Philippians* (Grand Rapids: Eerdmans, 1991).

O'Brien, P. T.,   'The Gospel and Godly Models in Philippians', in *Worship, Theology and Ministry in the Early Church. Essays in Honor of Professor Ralph P. Martin*, ed. M. J. Wilkins and T. Paige (Sheffield: Academic Press, 1992), 273-284.

O'Brien, P. T.,   'The Importance of the Gospel in Philippians', in *God who is Rich in Mercy. Essays presented to D. B. Knox*, ed. P. T. O'Brien and D. G. Peterson (Homebush West, NSW: Lancer, 1986), 213-233.

Pedersen, S.,   'Theologische Überlegungen zur Isagogik des Römerbriefes', *ZNW* 76 (1985), 47-67.

Peterson, D. G.,   *Engaging with God. A biblical theology of worship* (Leicester: IVP, Apollos, 1992).

Pfitzner, V. C.,   *Paul and the Agon Motif* (Leiden: Brill, 1967).

Polhill, J. B.,   'Paul: Theology Born of Mission', *RevExp* 78 (1981), 233-247.

Radl, W.,   'Alle Mühe umsonst? Paulus und der Gottesknecht', in *L'Apôtre Paul*, ed. A. Vanhoye (Leuven: Leuven UP, 1986), 144-149.

Radl, W.,   'Kult und Evangelium bei Paulus', *BZ* 31 (1987), 58-75.

Richardson, P.,   'Pauline Inconsistency: I Corinthians 9.19-23 and Galatians 2.11-14', *NTS* 26 (1979-80), 347-362.

Robertson, A. T., *A Grammar of the Greek New Testament in the Light of Historical Research* (Nashville: Broadman, 1934).

Robertson, A., and

Plummer, A.,   *A Critical and Exegetical Commentary on the First Epistle of St Paul to the Corinthians* (Edinburgh: Clark, ^{2}1914).

Robinson,   'The Priesthood of Paul in the Gospel of Hope', in
D. W. B.,   *Reconciliation and Hope. New Testament Essays on Atonement and Eschatology presented to L. L. Morris on his 60th Birthday*, ed. R. J. Banks (Exeter: Paternoster, 1974), 231-245.

Sandnes, K. O.,   *Paul—One of the Prophets?* (Tübingen: Mohr, 1991).

Satake, A.,   'Apostolat und Gnade bei Paulus', *NTS* 15 (1968-69), 96-107.

Schlier, H.,   'Εὐαγγέλιον im Römerbrief', in *Wort Gottes in der Zeit*, ed. K. Feld and J. Nolte (Dusseldorf: Patmos, 1973), 127-142.

Schnackenburg, R., *The Epistle to the Ephesians* (Edinburgh: Clark, 1991).

Schütz, J. H.,   *Paul and the Anatomy of Apostolic Authority* (Cambridge: Cambridge University Press, 1975).

Scobie, C. H. H., 'Jesus or Paul? The Origin of the Universal Mission of the Christian Church', in *From Jesus to Paul. Studies in Honour of F. W. Beare*, ed. P. Richardson and J. C. Hurd (Waterloo, Ontario: Wilfrid Laurier University, 1984), 47-60.

Senior, D. and   *Biblical Foundations for Mission* (London: SCM, 1983).
Stuhlmueller, C.,

Stanley, D. M.,   'Imitation in Paul's Letters: Its Significance for His Relationship to Jesus and to His Own Christian

Foundations', *From Jesus to Paul. Studies in Honour of Francis Wright Beare*, ed. P. Richardson and J. C. Hurd (Waterloo, Ontario: Wilfred Laurier University, 1984),127-141.

Stendahl, K., 'The Apostle Paul and the Introspective Conscience of the West', first published in 1963, now reprinted in *Paul among Jews and Gentiles* (Philadelphia: Fortress, 1977), 78-96.

Stolz, F., 'Zeichen und Wunder. Die prophetische Legitimation und ihre Geschichte', *ZTK* 69 (1972), 125-144.

Stott, J. R. W., *God's New Society. The Message of Ephesians* (Leicester: Inter-Varsity, 1979).

Stuhlmacher, P., *Das paulinische Evangelium. I. Vorgeschichte* (Göttingen: Vandenhoeck, 1968).

Stuhlmacher, P., 'The Pauline Gospel', in *Gospel and the Gospels*, ed. P. Stuhlmacher (Grand Rapids: Eerdmans, 1991), 149-172.

Stuhlmacher, P., 'The Theme: The Gospel and the Gospels', in *The Gospel and the Gospels*, 1-25.

Swartley, W. M., 'Biblical Perspectives for Mission', in *Mission Focus. Current Issues,* ed. W. Schenk and A. F. Glasser (Scottdale, PA: Herald, 1980), 17-28.

Turner, N., *Grammatical Insights into the New Testament* (Edinburgh: Clark, 1965).

Wedderburn, A. J. M.,*The Reasons for Romans* (Edinburgh: Clark, 1988).

Wiederkehr, D., *Die Theologie der Berufung in den Paulusbriefen* (Freiburg, Schweiz: Universitätsverlag, 1963).

Wiener, C., 'Ἱερουργεῖν (Röm 15:16)', *SPCIC* 2, 399-404.

Wikenhauser, A., *Pauline Mysticism. Christ in the Mystical Teaching of St. Paul* (London: Nelson, 1960).

Wilckens, U., *Die Brief an die Römer* 3 Vols. (Zürich: Benziger/Neukirchen: Neukirchener Verlag, 1978-1982).

Williams, S. K., 'The "Righteousness of God" in Romans', *JBL* 99 (1980), 241-290.

Woodhouse, J. W.,'Signs and Wonders in the Bible', in *Signs & Wonders and Evangelicals*, ed. R. Doyle (Homebush West, NSW: Lancer, 1987), 17-35.

Wright, N. T., 'The Messiah and the People of God. A Study in Pauline Theology with Particular Reference to the

	Argument of the Epistle to the Romans' (unpublished D. Phil. dissertation, Oxford, 1980).
Zeller, D.,	*Juden und Heiden in der Mission des Paulus* (Stuttgart: Katholisches Bibelwerk, 1976).
Zeller, D.,	'Theologie der Mission bei Paulus', in *Mission im Neuen Testament*, ed. K. Kertelge (Freiburg/Basel/Wien: Herder, 1982), 164–189.
Zmijewski, J.,	*Paulus—Knecht und Apostel Christi. Amt und Amtsträger in paulinischer Sicht* (Stuttgart: Katholisches Bibelwerk, 1986).

Index of Names

INDEX OF SCRIPTURE